Dancing
on Ice

Dancing on Ice

Jeremy Scott

OLD STREET PUBLISHING

First published in 2008 by Old Street Publishing Ltd
28-32 Bowling Green Lane, London EC1R 0BJ
www.oldstreetpublishing.co.uk

ISBN 978 1 90587 50 1

Grateful acknowledgement is made to the estate of Spencer Chapman and to the Scott Polar
Research Institute for kind permission to reproduce photographs from their collections. The
majority of pictures are taken from the Scott family archives. Every effort has been made to
trace copyright holders for the remaining illustrations, but in the event of an omission the
publisher should be contacted.

10 9 8 7 6 5 4 3 2 1

A CIP catalogue record for this title is available from the British Library.

Typeset by Old Street Publishing.
Printed and bound in Great Britain by Clays Ltd, St Ives plc.

For Jamie

Contents

Author's Note

The members of the Air-Route Expedition used the word 'Eskimo' (with no derogatory intent) to describe the people of Greenland in their conversations and journals. As *Dancing on Ice* draws so heavily on these primary sources, I felt that to shuttle between 'Eskimo' and 'Inuit' (a frequently misused term in itself) would spoil the immediacy of the narrative. I would like to assure readers that no disrespect is intended.

I have always been fascinated by danger... I love living dangerously, but as I am very easily frightened, and I dislike being frightened, I have always gone out of my way to do adventurous things in order to drive out fear and develop confidence in my ability to overcome my lack of courage. One can do this on the mental – or do I mean moral? – sphere. You agree, perhaps by just saying the one word 'yes' to do a certain thing.

F. Spencer Chapman, *Living Dangerously*

Without the instinct for adventure... any civilisation, however enlightened, any state, however well ordered, must wilt and wither.

Professor G. M. Trevelyan

INTRODUCTION

Risk has a bad name today. The bodies that govern our lives do all they can to protect us, and especially our children, from it. Yet some people, both young and old, find everyday life, if only at times, mundane and unsatisfactory. They crave more, a greater intensity – and they discover it in the adrenalin rush found in challenge, risk and going to the edge.

It was no desire for celebrity that drove Gino Watkins (my uncle) and J. M. Scott (my father) to the Arctic, but a taste for danger. My father says they were 'hooked' on it. It is not fanciful to compare risk to a drug, for this and the desire for a more exalted state are the symptoms of addiction.

I was born in 1934, two years after the return of the Air-Route Expedition, and as I grew up I could observe the effects of that addiction both on my father and on the other members of the party. For Father, the war created an ideal opportunity not just to satisfy his taste for adventure, hardship and danger, but also to teach it to others. As chief instructor at Lochailort Castle in the Scottish Highlands, the Special Operations Executive's school of unorthodox and 'ungentlemanly' warfare, he was responsible for training agents (both men and women) in survival, explosives, silent killing, and armed and unarmed combat.

Training was the same for both sexes. When it was completed they were smuggled into occupied territories by parachute or submarine, equipped with the explosives, devices and arms required to inflict maximum damage and disruption on the enemy. Early in the war Father believed what was inexpressible at that time: that Britain might be defeated and become an occupied country. To deal with this eventuality he 'liberated' an arsenal of weaponry, kept it in our home, and taught me how to use it, along with the rest of his trainees' curriculum. Before my teens I knew how to find my way cross-country at night; to bivouac and sleep out whatever the weather; to subsist without fire on limpets and mussels gathered on the shore and eaten raw. I was educated in knife work and garrotting, in how to blow up a bridge, derail a train with my bunched-up overcoat and break a man's windpipe with a rolled newspaper. All were skills a growing lad needed to possess, Father believed. And how delighted I was to acquire them in that rainswept landscape of mountain, loch and wilderness, where the only sound was the lonely cry of the curlew and distant rattle of small-arms' fire in the glen. Throughout my childhood I was blissfully and entirely happy.

In Greenland the air-route explorers had lived like the Inuit, by hunting seals, fishing and shooting. In Britain during the war food was short and rationing strict: we were always hungry. The skills Father taught me proved very useful. My initial response on shooting a living creature – horrified awe, dismay and revulsion – made me resolve on the walk home with the dead duck never to do so again. Yet at dinner that night, while the family sat at table enjoying a rare good meal, that feeling morphed into satisfaction, pride even, that I was the hunter who had brought home the meat. From then on, throughout the war, I shot, fished for trout and salmon with a rod (and occasionally a looted hand-grenade) as provider to my small family tribe.

Besides my father, four other members of the expedition, all of whom I knew as a teenager, worked for the Special Operations Executive (SOE). One of them, Spencer Chapman, spent three and a half years in the Malayan jungle behind Japanese lines wreaking extensive destruction on the enemy, for which he was awarded the DSO and Bar. For many of those Arctic men, the war provided the risks and highs their nature required. Only one, Courtauld, was different from the rest. I recall him as quiet, self-contained, apart.

What he had endured, alone on the ice-cap for five months – for six weeks buried in darkness beneath it – had taken him to another spiritual dimension, a separateness of the spirit from which I think he had neither desire nor motive to return.

For my father and those other members of the expedition who survived the war, its end confronted them with a peacetime life for which they were temperamentally unsuited. The real problem with drugs comes when you can't get them. Adventure and risk became ever harder to obtain. Courtauld went to his own stoic end; others declined in health and spirit; two shot themselves. For Father, the symptoms of withdrawal were misanthropy and drink.

The Arctic, which had made these men what they were and provided their greatest happiness, also ruined them. They had wanted more than everyday reality could provide, and in the Arctic they had found it. There they had lived to the full – and nothing could ever be that good again.

Among the readers of this true tale, a few no doubt already understand something of what drove them to that place.

Jeremy Scott

Buried Alive

At the heart of the floating iceberg is the body of a man, flash-frozen in the prime of his youth.

The iceberg containing him is the size of a four-storey house. Once it formed part of the vast ice sheet almost two miles thick that covered Greenland. Deepening under centuries of snowfall, it crept with infinite slowness toward the coast, was squeezed between mountains into rivers of solid ice and slithered down towards the sea. Eventually it reached the land's edge, protruded, protruded further, and calved. With a thunderous crash a giant mass split from its parent glacier and tumbled into the sea below, drifting south on the current toward the shipping lanes of the Atlantic.

Flawlessly preserved, the man encased in the ice is a perfect specimen of his type and period. A clean-cut young Englishman circa 1930, he belongs to a species on the verge of extinction. This particular example has been frozen for present study still wearing the shirt he has had on for a thousand years; a shirt which he bought at Harrods.

THAT WAS HIS destiny, that was how it would be if they didn't find him soon. The notion fastens on the man's mind as he lies waiting for them to come, and the flame of life within him dwindles to an ember for there seems no hope, no chance they can ever find him beneath the spreading white immensity which is his frozen home today, 5 May 1931. He is in a small tent 8,500 feet up on Greenland's ice cap, the most hostile landscape on earth. Alone.

The man has lived here in solitude for five months, most of the time in darkness. In all that period he has seen no one and heard no human voice, for he is without a radio and has no link to the outside world. In the barren wilderness stretching for countless miles about him he has glimpsed no growing thing, no beast, bird or insect, no colour and no sign of life. Embedded in that gigantic frozen slab creeping toward the sea, he is not on the ice cap but within it. The tent that forms his home is now completely buried except for a few inches of ventilation pipe poking above the surface of a vast ocean of storm-tossed snow. He has been here since 6 December; two days later the sun failed to rise above the horizon and the Arctic winter shut in an unremitting night. Blizzards rage continuously, the anemometer records windspeeds of 130mph, the thermometer a temperature of -41°C. The tunnel forming the exit to his burrow is blocked, frozen solid beneath a heavy drift of snow he cannot shift. For the last six weeks he has been trapped in his dark hole unable to get out.

At the start meals gave punctuation to the day; now his supply of food is almost gone, little paraffin remains. Each morning he heats up a small saucepan of porridge for breakfast – as he does today, hunched in his sleeping bag to tend the Primus. For weeks he has subsisted on only half rations. His body has grown thin, the muscles in his legs are wasted from lack of exercise. He can feel strength ebbing from him daily; only his will keeps him sane, his purpose to survive and pass on the all-important weather records he has maintained. Now most of the time he lies in his damp sleeping bag in darkness, lighting a candle only for minutes to keep up his diary or read a few sentences from a book. Sometimes he picks up and fondles the pipe given him by Mollie, the woman in England he had hoped to marry. Occasionally, very occasionally, he smokes it, luxuriating in the old homely fragrance and the memories it recalls. He is on his last tin of tobacco. 'I am completely buried. Paraffin has nearly run out and things are generally pretty dismal', he writes in his diary.

In his frozen den he crouches by the Primus, stirring watery gruel in the saucepan over a spluttering flame. Cooking this one meal is his only activity of the day; since the exit has become blocked he's been unable to continue his readings of the weather instruments outside. He has nothing else to do but think. Fears gnaw at his mind. The ventilator pipe will become obstructed with ice, the air in his lair grow toxic and poison him. Under the weight of snow the buried tent creaks and sags, it will give way and crush him beneath it. *Why has Gino not come for him? What has gone wrong?* The level of snow outside is now almost to the top of the tent; even if a relief party manages to get through to look for him, how will they find him? What in God's name is he doing imprisoned beneath the ice in this forsaken spot? Why is he here? Of all those insistent questions he knows the answer only to the last. He is here because he's chosen to be so. He came here 'to do something big'.

Now a further horror floods his mind. His home, this flimsy pod of air sunk into the ice cap, is *shrinking.* At first he tells himself it is paranoia, but he's taken measurements. His burrow has grown smaller; the tent has shrunk in size, its walls are bulging inward beneath the weight of snow compressing them. The roof is clustered with icicles, its canvas black with grime from the oil lamp. He has not had a bath or clean clothes for five months and his lair is a squalid stinking pit. For the last six weeks he's been unable to dispose of his own body waste.

On Easter Sunday, 5 April, there is only a cupful of paraffin remaining and two candles. He's finished the chocolate. His tobacco is almost gone; on 13 April he smokes his last pipeful. 'There is now precious little to live for,' he notes in his diary. On 20 April he lights his last candle. On 26 April only two biscuits remain. He is smoking tea leaves. Only half a cup of paraffin is left; there will be no way to melt snow for drinking water when it is ended. On 1 May he finishes the final biscuit. A little pemmican and some oatmeal remain but later that same day the stump of the last candle burns out. For the following four days he lies in cold, continual dark. Now on 5 May, as he kneels over the saucepan heating porridge for his breakfast, the jets of the Primus falter, splutter... and expire. The last of the paraffin has gone.

No fuel, no light, no hot food, nothing to smoke. No drinking water, only ice to suck and the weather station buried. Beneath him a layer of ice 8,500 feet deep, above and around him almost a million square miles of snow-covered desolation where nothing lives. Entombed beneath the ice cap, it is his 149th day of solitude. He is more alone than anyone on earth...

BLANK ON THE MAP

The scene is best imagined as a sepia photograph, a picture postcard of the period, faded and chafed at the edges. Depicting a view of London at the end of the 1920s, it shows a wide road, Kensington Green, wonderfully free of traffic. What there is amounts to no more than three box-shaped cars or cabs, all of them black – the largest driven by a chaffeur in peaked cap – and a goods dray pulled by a pair of carthorses clopping toward the West End with its load of wooden barrels. On the far side of the road, which is separated by ornamental railings from the trees and cropped grass of Kensington Gardens, a small girl in Alice-in-Wonderland dress and leggings, accompanied by her nanny, is guiding a hoop along the pavement by an iron wand hooked to its rim. On *this* side of the street stands a large Victorian mansion of dark red brick. At the bottom of this imposing edifice, and only just visible in the photograph, the figure of a uniformed housemaid can be spotted emerging from her basement area with a dustpan and shovel to gather up the small pile of manure which one of the passing horses has just deposited in the road. Despite the sunlit day, the appearance of the red-brick mansion is rather forbidding:it looks like what it is, the home of a venerable institution existing since 1830. It is the Royal Geographical Society.

On this spring morning one of the upper windows in the building's gloomy façade is wide open. From it is coming loud jazz music. The sound of Louis Armstrong's *West End Blues* reaches across the road into the leafy park where a nursemaid pushing a baby in a high perambulator picks up her step on hearing it while for a moment her attention strays from her duty in a quick glance toward the source of that syncopated beat.

Inside the room where the music is playing a blond young man, faultlessly dressed in a grey flannel suit, stands by the wind-up gramophone, talking and laughing with two others. Beyond them, a further group lounging around a trestle table have abandoned all pretence of work and are chatting together exuberantly. The room, with its upright wooden chairs, shelves of leather-bound books and maps and metal filing cabinet in the corner, looks like an office. But the young men in their sports jackets and ties do not have the appearance of office workers; their manner and the way they are behaving suggests that, despite the early hour, this is a party. In fact, the atmosphere in this room over the last few weeks has always been high-spirited and noisy, but today the mood of the group is almost manic. And it has every reason to be so. Today the last brick has fallen into place and the dream finally become reality. They have just learned that the expedition to the Arctic put together by Gino Watkins is definitely *on,* a goer.

The idea had come to Gino the year before when he had been in Labrador with his friend, J. M. Scott. They were travelling by canoe and dog sledge to map the head waters of Hamilton River in an unexplored area of the country.

Both men were the same age (twenty-two), but their personalities were very different, as was their appearance. Gino, slight and fair, with a taste for jazz, dancing and sports cars, did not fit most people's idea of an explorer; a fellow undergraduate remarked that he looked like a 'pansy'. In contrast to his rather effete figure, Scott was broad-shouldered, muscular and dark-haired; he had won a rugby Blue at Cambridge and shown himself good in the scrum. Rather less good off the field, for he was emotionally reserved, serious minded and a little uncomfortable with people he didn't know. Yet what had brought the two men together was enough to override all disparity between them, for they shared a consuming passion. Perhaps it was more compelling than passion (Scott would describe it later as an 'addiction'); they were both hooked on the combination of extreme adventure and the unknown.

Risk in various forms is accessible today, but seventy-five years ago that *particular* compound was more readily available. There still were unknown places in the world, places no one had yet gone to; there were blanks on the map. It was no desire for fame that drew them to those untrodden regions but something visceral and instinctive to their nature. They had tasted it already; both had known the high of venturing into that vast, white, empty landscape of cruel beauty and truth. To face the adversities they encountered there required comradeship, resolution and courage. Their existence was harsh but simple and their purpose clear. They were fully alive there; it was a place of elemental purity in a messy and uncertain world.

Gino and Scott wanted more of it. They craved the exhilaration of challenge and adventure – but neither of them had a penny to his name. How could they raise the cash for another and bigger expedition to the Arctic? One night in their shared tent in Labrador Gino came up with the answer: the Arctic Air-Route Expedition. The future of travel lay in the air, so they should tap into the spirit of the age and open up a flight path between Europe and America.

Two years before, in 1927, Charles Lindbergh had made the first solo flight from New York to Paris in 33½ hours, winning a $25,000 prize. But to achieve that 3,000-mile ocean crossing he had been unable to carry anything except fuel. Transatlantic passenger travel continued exclusively by ocean liner and airship, as before. But, as Gino reasoned to Scott in that sealed tent dense with pipe smoke, if one traced the great circle route from the British Isles to North America there existed stepping-stones where a plane could land to refuel. And each hop between these stones was less than 500 miles, so a commercial passenger route was possible. Theoretically.

'It is certain,' Gino wrote in his diary, 'that nearly all the great air routes of the future will lie across the Arctic. The safest and quickest air route from England to the American continent is by Iceland, Greenland and Labrador... But before anything can be done, these places must be scientifically explored...' Gino's idea was prescient at the time; viewed from today it looks obvious. 1929 was a seminal year in the infancy of the airline business when four of the players who would dominate the trade first entered the market. Tom Braniff opened a single route from Tulsa to Oklahoma City, with two rickety aircraft piloted by himself and his younger brother. The National Airlines Taxi Service (later shortened to National Airlines) acquired a 142-mile mail route from St Petersburg to Daytona Beach. United Airlines was formed, using Ford Tri-Motor planes to cut flying time from New York to San Francisco to twenty-eight hours. And Howard Hughes, movie producer and aviator, started TWA with a government mail contract.

Thirty-six years later Hughes would sell his shares for $500 million, but at the time many thought his stake worthless. Airlines were struggling to survive, none was making money. And all for the same reason. The public was scared to death of flying, and with good cause. Airplanes were primitive, draughty crates; their instruments were basic and navigation elementary; they caught fire or iced-up. All in all, flying was a chancy business. For those early airlines naked fear among the customer-base was a major marketing problem. The movie *Hell's Angels* (produced by Howard Hughes) had just been released and was showing to big audiences in the US and Britain. Sensational and spectacular, it featured nausea-inducing footage of open-cockpit stunt flying and several lives had been lost in the making of it. Air travel was seen as glamorous, exciting… and dangerous.

Airships were thought much safer. And not just safer but infinitely more roomy, comfortable and luxurious, of far greater appeal to wealthy men and women accustomed to the pampered opulence of transatlantic liners. You didn't have to wrap up in greatcoat and scarf to travel on an airship, where uniformed stewards served you a five-course dinner and vintage wines. Airships were the airlines' well-established rivals, and they dominated the market. Fixed-wing airplanes looked particularly fallible when in January 1929 Imperial's airliner *City of Ottowa* developed engine trouble on a flight from London to Paris and came down in the English Channel, drowning seven. In contrast the *Graf Zeppelin* airship flew serenely from the US to Europe in 55½ hours that August, then continued its voyage in an attempt to fly around the world. Twenty-one days later it landed at Lakehurst, New Jersey after a successful journey of 21,000 miles. In November *Airship R101* completed her final test flight with eighty-two people on board, the largest number ever carried by a British dirigible.

Then came disaster. On the R101's maiden voyage to India, with a full complement of passengers, the craft caught fire and crashed in France, killing fifty-four people. A few years later, the giant *Hindenberg* (804 feet in length, the largest and finest airship ever built) burst into flame while landing at Lakehurst, New Jersey, incinerating all thirty-six passengers and the crew. In that fireball of blazing hydrogen the *Hindenberg*, and with it the whole airship industry, burned to ash in minutes – leaving the future to the airlines.

To raise money to go to the Arctic they should tap into that future, Gino proposed to Scott. And during the rest of their time in Labrador the two continued to discuss the feasibility of an expedition to pioneer an air route from London to North America across Greenland's ice cap. When they got back to London that autumn Gino started to draft a proposal to put before the Royal Geographical Society (RGS), whose seal of approval they would require before they could attempt to raise funds, equipment and supplies.

On their return to England, the RGS lent them that room overlooking the park which would later become the Air-Route Expedition's office. Here the two of them worked out the astro-nomical observations they had taken in Labrador and transcribed their rough survey notes for the draughtsmen who would use them to redraw the territory's map and boundary. Scott describes the scene:

> There, during nearly two months, he and I sat in short sleeves at a trestle-table drawn up to the open window. One morning Gino brought a Japanese fan, which he had looted from a dance the night before. He leaned back, fanning himself and gazing out of the window whenever he stopped to recall some incident of a journey of which the survey notes reminded him; and he always kept the fan beside him 'so that,' he said, 'I can give the right impression if anyone very tough and hearty comes to see me.'

Gino had always enjoyed teasing the rugger buggers and the ultra-respectable. It amused him to play the affected poser and he liked to shock, but his manner concealed a ruthless, fully-focused will.

'If a man wants anything badly enough he can get it, absolutely anything,' he told Scott.

An expedition surveying an air route over the ice cap would need to include a light aircraft among its equipment, ideally with a second plane as back-up. Gino had learnt to fly in the Cambridge Air Squadron while at university, but during his first lesson in map-making and aerial photography the plane had crashed. Gino, who was standing up in the open cockpit at the time clutching the survey camera, was thrown clear as the aircraft struck the ground and flipped over onto its back, but the pilot was left suspended upside down in his harness. Gino scrambled back to the plane still holding the camera, delighted by what had happened. He hoped his instructor didn't mind him saying so, but it was an experience he was very glad to have had. Releasing the embarrassed pilot, he insisted he pose for a photograph standing on top of the wreckage, a hunter with his kill.

On his return from Labrador Gino joined the Auxiliary Airforce in order to gain a pilot's certificate. The small wage he received was useful in paying for drinks at London nightclubs, for he was living on a small and rather irregular allowance from his father, Colonel Watkins. His mother had killed herself just before Gino's Labrador expedition. His sister Pam (twenty) and brother Tony (seventeen) lived together in a house on Onslow Crescent, Kensington, looked after by a resident cook and Nanny Dennis, who had brought up all three children and who would remain with the family until her death. There was no money coming in. Harrods' and tradesmen's bills were sent to Colonel Watkins in Switzerland, who forwarded them to his elderly mother in Florence to settle.

Onslow Crescent was Gino's home when in England. Almost every morning in the autumn of 1929, he was woken early to dress in the clothes Nanny had brushed and laid out for him, grab a quick breakfast and set off in his old Lagonda to Stag Lane airfield. At the flying club there was usually a group of people drinking coffee and playing darts and table tennis while waiting for their turn to fly. Gino did not join in. He would arrive, dressed as for the City with bowler hat, tightly rolled umbrella and attaché case, and sit down to work in a quiet corner of the room. When the weather was fit and an airplane available he pulled on a helmet and flying suit, spent an hour or two in the air and then went back to his expedition papers. His instructors laughed at first; they were later to be disarmed, but all remained puzzled by this immaculate and self-contained young man. What his fellow students thought of him is not known but may be imagined.

Gino deliberately included Pam and Scott in his social evenings out, for they knew almost no one in London. And London was *fun* then – fun in a way that would not be seen again until the sixties. In both periods it was music that set the mood. There were parties every night: cocktail, costume, swimming pool or bottle parties. Someone always knew of one taking place somewhere. Gino was mad about jazz, night-clubs, dancing. 'It was not that he was extravagant,' says Scott. 'He was quite the reverse, for he had a very shrewd sense of values which enabled him to live and travel more cheaply than most people and to enjoy the achievement of doing so. Tangible possessions like books and pictures meant very little to Gino and he wasted nothing on them… But memories meant a great deal: memories he could take with him and enjoy on any journey, however lightly he was travelling. He was a rich collector of experiences.'

Becoming an explorer had occurred at a timely moment for Gino, as he was due to leave Cambridge in less than a year, probably with a poor degree. He would have to get a job and he had not the faintest idea what. It was a bad time to find one and his contemporaries' plans to enter the City, the services, or go into business struck him as infinitely unappealing. He had no particular desire for wealth or any identifiable ambition to motivate him. He wanted excitement and adventure; a nine-to-five routine looked to him a secure grave. The idea of a job and of working his way up in a business held no attraction. 'It was not because he was afraid of hard or menial work,' says Scott, 'But because he could not appreciate the virtue of promotion by seniority rather than initiative. Experience was the most valuable possession, but its collection was an active, varied business entirely different from slow plodding. He often said one must have done everything by the age of twenty-five.'

For ten months in Labrador, Scott and Gino had shared adventures, dangers and hunger. At night they slept in the same small tent. Since returning to England they had shared an office and a mutual project, and gone to the same parties. Yet Scott says:

> Often when I was a member of these parties I discovered some unexpected trait of Gino's character; and so I was surprised when people told me that I must have got to know him wonderfully well in Labrador. To a limited extent I had... I knew that I could trust him in an emergency. The more we did together the more firmly we were connected... but we did not even grow sufficiently demonstrative to call each other by our Christian names.

Ever since his return from Labrador, Gino had been working on, and talking to, suitable people; selling his vision of an air-route expedition. By now these plans were sufficiently advanced to be presented as a formal proposal to the Royal Geographical Society:

> I am anxious to study the practicability of an Air Route from England to the Pacific coast of America, via Iceland, Greenland, Baffin Land, Hudson Bay and Edmonton...

The part of this route which is least known at present is the East Coast and central ice plateau of Greenland which is almost entirely unmapped, and very little is known of the meteorological conditions on the ice cap...

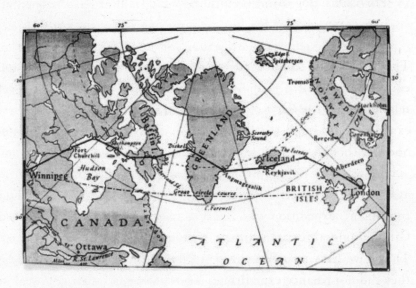

The planned path of the air route, the first to link Europe with America

The expedition would remain in Greenland for one year. It would be equipped with two airplanes, a couple of motor-boats and a large number of dog teams for hauling sledges. Its aims were: 1. To establish a weather station on the ice cap in the centre of the country where meteorological observations could be recorded throughout the year. 2. To use airplanes, motor-boats and sledges to carry out a detailed survey of Greenland's east coast, and to establish the height of the coastal mountains. 3. To test flying and landing conditions in the Arctic, and at the end of the year make a flight with the two planes along the proposed air route.

Gino's estimate of the cost of the expedition was £12,000, based on:

Charter of ship	£1,500
Two suitable aeroplanes, spare parts, petrol, etc.	£3,500
Wages to pilots and mechanics	£2,000
Provisions: dog teams, equipment, hut for the base camp, etc.	£5,000

The sum of £12,000 seems ludicrously small, but it was the equivalent of half a million pounds today. Gino enjoyed a good relationship with the Royal Geographical Society. After his first expedition to Edge Island he had been elected a Fellow of the Society, though as the President explained at the award ceremony 'There was one slight difficulty in that (at twenty) he was under age.' He had also been awarded a grant, all of which he had spent on funding his expedition with Scott to Labrador. The RGS examined Gino's proposal for an air route expedition and endorsed his plans. They gave him an office to use while setting it up but no funds; they did not finance expeditions. The project had their gold seal of approval, but it was up to him to raise the money. The New York stock market had just crashed, triggering a worldwide depression. This was the worst moment imaginable to try to raise money for anything, let alone a trip to some place called Greenland.

Gino and Scott sat at the trestle table in their room in the RGS writing letters to accompany the proposal, which they mailed to manufacturers of the wide range of equipment and supplies they needed. To make clothing, boots, tents, skis, surveying equipment, or produce margarine or canned meat, is a useful and worthy job, but it is just possibly a little dull. One imagines that the expedition proposal must have rung a strange chime in some of the chief executives and managing directors who read it on a grey morning in a musty city office at a time when business was terrible. Most of the people they wrote to invited them to visit. Once there, the pair's track record and obvious professionalism, combined with Gino's singular brand of charm, usually did the rest. Equipment and supplies were assured, but cash was harder.

One morning a letter delivered to the room in the RGS contained a proposition from a movie company wishing to shoot a feature film in the Arctic. They proposed a deal: Gino's expedition party would include their director, film crew and cast. In return for the explorers' help in shooting the action sequences the movie company would subscribe to the finances of the expedition. Gino was initially entranced by the idea. He relished absurdity, it added a comic grace-note to life. Besides, it would shock the establishment and that was always fun. Scott says he held the most fabulous ideas about Hollywood: 'That the women were exotic in their beauty and erotic in their way of life, and the men green of complexion, prodigal and sinister.'

The explorer/movie producer collaboration progressed through several meetings. A screenplay was written with a strong love interest, and a shooting schedule drawn up which included such sequences as: *Blizzard Scenes, Trouble with dogs* and *Loss of two of the party (members of the Expedition lost down a crevasse).* Two reasons caused Gino finally to reject the idea. The surveying and mapping of the mountain ranges on Greenland's east coast, which represented an unknown hazard to any air route, had to be completed before the storms and darkness of Arctic winter. Time could not be lost in film-making, whatever fun it promised, and there was another consideration. To take an expedition to Greenland would require permission from the Danish government, who were opposed to any influence which risked modernising the Eskimos. The spectacle of Hollywood disporting like Hollywood on the ice cap could well provide a culture shock from which they might never recover.

So Gino looked elsewhere for funding. His own family had no money, as his father had wasted it all on foolish schemes and restless living, but many of his relations were rich. Some subscribed, but he needed major funds to make the project a reality. The treasurer to the would-be Arctic Air-Route Expedition was August Courtauld. Three years older than Gino, he too had been at Cambridge, though they had not met there. After graduating, Courtauld had gone to work for a City stockbroker, a job he detested. Very soon after Gino started to formulate his plans for the Air-Route Expedition he had asked to become a member of the party. Courtauld already had Arctic experience. He also knew how to fly and held a pilot's licence. He was a useful addition to the group and Gino was glad to accept him. The two had background in common: both were by nature anti-establishment and anti-authority, and each had fitted in badly at public school, where they had been notably unsuccessful. But the circumstances of the two could scarcely have been more contrasting. Gino penniless; Courtauld rich and potentially very very rich, for he was heir to the family textile fortune.

August's father, Samuel Courtauld, was a millionaire and a natural mark for expedition funds. But he was a practical businessman lacking in romantic imagination, and he did not enjoy a particularly good relationship with his son. Nevertheless a plan was concocted, and Gino was duly invited to the family's country estate to shoot. Driving down in the ancient and chronically infirm Lagonda, he arrived in the middle of the shooting party and August offered to lend him a gun, but Gino held up a right hand swathed in bandages, asking to be excused because he had sprained his thumb. He passed his day as a spectator, had his conversation with Samuel Courtauld in the evening and drove home to be greeted by the anxious enquiries of his family who did not know that he had hurt himself. 'Oh my hand's alright,' said Gino, peeling off the bandage, 'But I couldn't afford to tip the gamekeeper.'

However, Samuel Courtauld proved unsusceptible to Gino's charm. He was implacably not won over and refused to subscribe a penny to the expedition. Suspecting his mother had been at work, August was disgusted.

> He wants me safe and stuck rather than run the risk that his family might ever get out of the rut of complacent money-making to bring a small spot of credit to this womanly old country of ours. I am so sick with my family I can't even sit with it. Let it fug in its own noxious library. If only I could rake up some of its slimy past and do some subtle blackmail on them...

Perhaps he did. 'I tackled the cousins and aunts... They stumped up nobly.' The most enthusiastic was his father's cousin, Stephen Courtauld, who became chairman of the expedition committee. Whether this idea was August's or Gino's is not known, but it proved a well-calculated piece of casting for it led to the sunlit happiness possessing that party of young men grouped around Gino's wind-up gramophone in the Royal Geographical Society, whose description forms the opening to this chapter. It is the news they have just received which has caused the thrill visible on the flushed faces of these chaps in tweed jackets and wide Oxford bags. The air is wreathed with pipe fumes, most are smoking hard and all are talking at the same time above the reedy sound of jazz coming from the Victrola. Looking at them, it is their youth that strikes you most. Some are still at university, the rest have just come down, but in this unguarded moment they look like boys. All have short hair, greased and combed flat; there's a sheen where the light catches it. Their tight jackets are creased and don't fit them very well. There's an artless air to them, an unselfconsciousness similar to that of children at play. Their faces are clear, fresh and healthy, and there's an expression in their eyes you don't see nowadays. It's hard to define it (in a moment, though not now, glance at their photographs and try), but there's an openness in their gaze, innocence perhaps, or hope. Hope certainly is running high in them today, hope no longer deferred but real and present. Their lives have been transformed. Their future is infinite in possibility and dazzling in a sparkle of fire and ice. This morning Stephen Courtauld's all-enabling cheque has come in with the mail. They have the green light. They are going to the Arctic.

THE JAZZ AGE

THAT CAREFREE GROUP surrounding Gino is penniless but privileged. Their advantages are undeniable, though looking back at them from this distance in time you are aware that the grace which favours them most particularly is due to the date of their birth. The twenties were the best of all times to be young.

The key to a period, the symbols characterising it which a film director employs to recreate an era long after it has passed into history, are, in the case of the twenties, the clothes, music and dancing. The taste for dancing was not new, it had started before World War I when swanky restaurants and hotels first hired orchestras to entertain their guests. The war democratised the trend, spreading it downmarket. Dancing suited the heightened emotions of wartime and the sentiments that fed its mood: escapism; the poignancy of love and parting; the dream of peace.

Then came that peace – and with it a startled awareness that the world had changed. The slaughter of ten million people across the globe had debunked established authority along with its traditions and moral code. A vast catharsis had taken place; now was the dawn to a new era. In mounting astonishment the young came to realise that it belonged to *them*, to make it how they would. In high exhilaration, they partied and they danced. In 1923 came radio, or 'wireless' as it was quaintly called, an object the size of a suitcase sprouting a trumpet, with a wire stretching to the roof for aerial and another earthing the contraption to a gas pipe. The piano solo *Kitten on the Keys* became the first musical number played in ragtime over the airwaves. A craze for dancing swept across the country, a mania seized the young and not-so-young and propelled them upon the crowded floor. They danced in hotels and restaurants, in nightclubs and dives, in dancehalls and pubs. They danced at teatime and between courses at dinner, then moved on to continue dancing elsewhere. They danced the one-step, the two-step, the quick-step, the fox-trot and the tango. Then the charleston arrived from America and the young threw off the last remnants of inhibition and let rip.

Outrage and affront were the reactions of the older generation. There were calls to prohibit the practice. A sign in the Hammersmith Palais de Danse read: YOU ARE EARNESTLY REQUESTED NOT TO DANCE THE CHARLESTON, providing great incentive to do so. The charleston was the cocky assertion of youth and a two-finger gesture to the rest. The charleston *belonged* to youth and excluded the old. You had to possess high energy and be fit to dance it. The old who were unwise or drunk enough to attempt to imitate them looked ridiculous, and risked collapsing from a heart attack.

Next, the Blackbirds Negro Revue arrived in London from New York, bringing with it the unchaste rhythms of the south: the black bottom and the shimmy, the mess-around and the grind. In Paris, Josephine Baker erupted onto the cabaret stage to prance before a startled audience, with nothing but glitterdust and a handful of bananas to cover her oiled black skin. To the atmosphere in these crowded venues, already redolent with expensive perfume and dense with cigarette smoke, was added a further fragrance: the pungent odour of sweating bodies. The effect upon some of the elegantly gowned women in the audience was similar to that of a rank aphrodisiac. These shows became a must-see, a must-see many times – the Prince of Wales saw the Blackbirds twenty times. Its cast, the stomping progeny of slaves, became the most sought-after guests in town. What an opportunity for sedition, what a cue to cock a snook and shock the world! Miscegenation became the height of chic, the *dernier cri*. The 'negro craze' was reported to have infected women in 'the highest ranks of society.' Lady Edwina Mountbatten – wife to bisexual Dickie, the Prince of Wales' closest pal – took Paul Robeson (the singer and civil rights activist) to her bed, then replaced him with Leslie 'Hutch' Hutchinson, the black pianist and singer. In Paris, Nancy Cunard, trendsetter to the avant-garde, was quick to accessorise herself with a black lover. Her mother Emerald, one of London's leading hostesses, was accosted by a boisterous Margot Asquith who burst into her party demanding loudly, 'Hello Emerald! What is it now, drink, drugs, or niggers?'

Not just black people but the exotic in general became popular additions to any gathering: entertainers, artists, dwarves – even homosexuals. Exquisite young men like Cecil Beaton, Brian Howard and Stephen Tennant with affected voices, languid manners and cruel wits became prized guests. Camp became an art-form in itself, even though homosexuality had been inadmissible before 1914. 'I thought men like that shot themselves,' said George V when told someone he knew was gay.

Yet homosexuals had long been tacitly accepted in Britain, if not acknowledged. Everyone knew a 'confirmed bachelor' or a maiden aunt of unbending rectitude who lived with a 'lady companion'. But now sapphism as well as homosexuality was daringly, openly expressed. Its apostles had short hair smoothed and parted like a man's, wore tuxedos, and defied the public's stare with a long cigarette holder clenched in a corner of the mouth. The more extreme sported a monocle and an expression of haughty challenge. The police, who regularly raided certain pubs where male gays congregated in an attempt to eradicate the perceived 'infection', were baffled by the newly fashionable transgression. They prosecuted the publishers of Radcliffe Hall's *Well of Loneliness*, but when they came face to face with the physical practices of the love that dare not speak its name, they were impotent; for, by the elderly males who had drafted the laws, such activity was not recognised to exist. With cool disdain the sapphist withdrew the cigarette holder from her scarlet lips to blow a thin jet of smoke full into Old Bill's indignant face.

What brave new world that has such people in it! The Jazz Age they called it, the Roaring Twenties. Movies, radio and leisure redefined the ethos. Habits changed, particularly women. Girls turned into 'flappers', they were seen to have legs and to bat their baby blues – as the expression went – beneath eyebrows plucked to a line. They smoked in public, drank cocktails, said, 'Go bag your face!' and discovered sex was 'fun'. 'If all the girls at the Yale prom were laid end to end,' said Dorothy Parker, 'I wouldn't be surprised.'

Young women wore artificial silk stockings and 'paint': lipstick, kohl and rouge. They bobbed their hair or wore it in shingles or an Eton crop under small tight hats of metallic cloth. Their shape altered: breasts and hips were out. Inspired by advertising, they smoked to lose weight (and 'to prevent sore throats'); they became boyish and sleek. Mothers were encouraged to smoke by their children who collected into sets the nifty card each pack contained. Sport further toned a girl's figure: tennis, athletics, swimming, skiing and golf. Advertising and mass communication had come into being and their influence was unstoppable. The machine and mass production set fashionable clothes before the public in an available feast. The installation of plate glass created a wholly new activity – window-shopping – and department stores became palaces of delight. This was the glorious dawn of consumer culture and a world we can recognise as our own.

That then is the scene, a description of the setting which forms the background to Gino and his group. A picture necessarily impressionistic and inadequate for it ignores the lives of 90 per cent of Britain's population who did *not* live like that because they were too poor, but only read about these doings in the papers or glimpsed them in newsreels at the local cinema, where a seat cost three pence.

This is the world that Gino and his party are soon to leave behind. On arrival in the Arctic they will survey a 500-mile air route across Greenland's unexplored ice cap; a route which the passenger airplanes of the day will take in a new, regular intercontinental service from Europe to America. It is an ambitious and – as some will say later when it goes wrong – a reckless plan.

Surrounded by 5½ million square miles of Arctic ocean, most of it frozen, Greenland's ice cap is a massive slab of compacted frozen snow nine times the size of Britain. It has built up over thousands of years, burying the entire country beneath a solid layer thought to be 9,000 feet thick – though nobody knew for sure in the early twentieth century as almost all of it was unmapped. Gino's plan was to map the coast and mountain ranges and a route across the country, but most crucially to set up a meteorological station high on the ice cap near the centre of Greenland, which, manned in shifts for one year, would record temperature, wind and weather conditions six times a day. No one before had ever passed a winter on the ice cap, but without this information a regular air service flying over the Arctic was out of the question.

Nobody on the expedition, or anywhere else, knew what to expect.

On the eastern shore of Greenland there were only two settlements, Angmagssalik and Scoresby Sound. The Eskimos inhabiting them roamed north and south along the coast in summer, fishing and hunting seals and seabirds. They kept to the shoreline of the fjords and did not stray inland onto that frozen desolation where nothing grew, no life existed and there was no game to hunt. They never ventured onto the ice cap. To them it was a zone of horror where the very ground was in motion, a fluid landscape constantly reshaping in the wind. A place of dread, shrieking blizzards and the home of devils.

Since the start of history the Arctic had been thought a region of terror. Even when the whaling and sealing industry was at its peak with scores of ships operating out of New England and northern Europe, the fear of endless night and the perils of ice so haunted the minds of sailors that they simply refused to remain there throughout the year. In the seventeenth century the English government offered a free pardon to a group of condemned prisoners under sentence of execution on condition that they would spend a winter in the Arctic. So appalled were they at the idea they refused, choosing death instead.

The Arctic, covering an area of more than five million square miles, was almost entirely unexplored until 1845 when Sir John Franklin, with 135 officers and men in two ships, the *Erebus* and *Terror*, sailed in search of the Northwest Passage linking the Atlantic to the Pacific around the top of the world. They disappeared. The Admiralty offered a reward of £20,000 to anyone finding the expedition. Many tried for it. In the year 1850, fifteen ships (Royal Navy, American Navy and privately funded) sailed north from the Pacific and Atlantic coasts to look for the lost party, but without success. Then in 1859 a stone cairn was discovered, and in it a report of Franklin's death. His ships had been held fast in the ice for two years before the remaing men set off, dragging boats with them across the ice, in a desperate trek to starvation, cannibalism and death. Though many ships that searched for the expedition found nothing, still the quest resulted in the eventual discovery of the Northwest Passage and the mapping of the Arctic archipelago.

At this moment when Gino is preparing to sail for the region, Greenland's precipitous east coast had been charted only superficially, while the country's inland waste remains a place of mystery. The map shows blank. There are few reports and a lack of published material. Other information required for the expedition is equally deficient. There are no manuals on cold weather survival, on dietary requirements in sub-zero temperatures, on sledging or the management of dog teams. And there exists almost no protective clothing in the sense we understand today; Gino climbed and skied in the Alps wearing a tweed jacket and tie, as did all who were in a position to enjoy the new sport.

Now, while recruiting the remaining members of the expedition, assembling equipment and stores, and searching for suitable aircraft and a ship to transport the party to the Arctic, Gino lived with his siblings Pam and Tony in the house they were renting in Onslow Crescent. They possessed almost no money, hardly a penny of income between the three of them. It was their familiar, their normal situation. Until recently, when their mother was still alive, they had existed in similar penury in another much grander house in Eaton Place. Their father Colonel Watkins, now living in Switzerland, had throughout his marriage shown an infallible instinct for a dud investment and soon lost the capital he had inherited. An officer in the Coldstream Guards, his regimental duties were undemanding. Domestic and family existence did not appeal to him, so he spent little time at home, enjoying an active life of travelling, skiing and hunting chamois in the Alps. Leaving the army at the age of forty, he became a King's Messenger. One of his early missions was to

Moscow, where he bought two half-grown bears which he shipped back to England as a present for his children. For weeks the pair occupied a cage in the hall in Eaton Place but unsurprisingly failed to become the cuddly pets he envisaged. Their ferocity terrified everybody; it was impossible to use the front door, and visitors and the family came and went via the basement area. The bears not only menaced any human who came near but fought each other savagely, making a fearsome noise unusual in Eaton Place whose well-heeled residents were unaccustomed to the sound of domestic conflict at any level. Yet no one complained. It got worse, for in the course of one particularly disorderly night the male bear solved the rivalry between them by murdering his sibling. Yet next day, when the still-raving victor was with difficulty negotiated out the house and into a caged van by a riot posse from the London Zoo, not a curtain twitched in Eaton Place.

Then Colonel Watkins contracted tuberculosis. An incurable disease at that time, mountain air was thought to be beneficial and he moved to a sanatorium specialising in the illness. His wife and children joined him for climbing and skiing holidays, staying in a nearby hotel. When they were not with him – which was most of the time – he led the cosseted life of an invalid, sitting in the sun in a deck chair with a rug across his legs. A charming, amusing though wholly unreasonable man, he took up with a glamorous Austrian, Countess Hoyös. After a time it became clear he would not be returning to England.

In Eaton Place his wife, Jennie, had found herself in impossible circumstances. She had the house, three children, Nanny and the servants to support, school and university bills to pay. For money she depended on intermittent cheques from her feckless husband's aged mother who lived in Florence. She complained to no one – only domestic servants ever complained – yet her husband's desertion, the bears in the hall and wolf at the door finally became too much for her. One morning she kissed her children goodbye and caught a train to Eastbourne. At the station she hired a taxi to take her to Beachy Head, a landmark headland with a vertiginous rockface plunging to the sea below. There she paid off the taxi and disappeared. Presumably she walked to the cliff's edge and jumped, but her body was never found.

While preparing to sail for Greenland, Gino and Scott spent their days at the Air-Route Expedition's office in the RGS assisted by the young men and women who had offered to help. Gino's research at this time was focused on food; he was trying to work out a diet which would best sustain men living and working for long periods in sub-zero temperatures and high altitude. He had studied the composition of the rations used by Captain Scott's party in the Antarctic during their attempt to reach the pole eighteen years before. These had proved ineffective. The group had lost strength and become increasingly susceptible to cold. Something more nutritious was needed for the ice cap.

The science of dietetics had moved on since then, though not far. Buying a sixpenny book on the subject, Gino swotted up on the ratio of fat, carbohydrates and protein in the ideal cold-weather diet, together with the essential vitamins. He decided that men working strenuously in these conditions needed 6,000 calories a day – a thousand more than Scott's party. These rations had to be minimal in bulk and concentrated so they weighed no more than thirty-six ounces. That was the problem.

During several weeks Gino experimented, finally arriving at a daily menu which seemed to fulfil those requirements. He took it to the Lister Institute for a scientific opinion. They agreed that the composition was theoretically efficient, but questioned whether a man could keep down and digest a diet one third of which was solid fat. Proof was needed, and Gino broke the news to a rather dismayed Scott that *they* would provide it: they were going to try living on it in London.

It was the height of the Season. The debutantes of that year had been presented at court. Now the parents of each were giving a dance designed to launch their daughter on the marriage market. Young men of the right sort were in demand, invited to two or three a night. Gino and Scott were on the list. Every evening they were asked to a pre-dance dinner party. They came dressed in white tie and tails, each clutching a package of pemmican (compressed fatty meat) and margarine which they took with them into dinner. Seated at table they unwrapped their personal menu – a fist-sized lump of impacted grease, as repulsive to look at as to taste – and forced themselves to eat, watched with appalled fascination by their fellow guests.

Gino found it funny, he loved to shock people, but Scott did not. He had never overcome his adolescent shyness, particularly with women, and for him it was a social as well as a physical ordeal. The food was nauseating, and even Gino found it hard to hold a conversation with the girl beside him while worrying he might throw up in her lap. But they kept their rations down and months later on the ice cap, lying in their sleeping-bags blissfully content after that same disgusting meal, they giggled at the memory of those nights of stomach-lurching horror.

In the office, Gino and Scott discussed dogs. They required huskies, at least fifty of them. The strongest were to be found in Labrador and on the west coast of Greenland. However, the idea of buying dozens of these half-savage beasts, somehow transporting them to the Faroe Islands and keeping them there till the expedition ship could pick them up, was daunting. 'I wonder if we could find a man who knows as much about sledge dogs as you do,' Gino mused aloud one day to Scott.

'Accepting the compliment, I could scarcely refuse,' Scott comments. He set off for west Greenland with a wad of local currency but some reservations about his brief to purchase and ship the brutes. Meanwhile Gino confirmed charter of the *Quest*, a 125-ton wooden sealing ship which had weathered both Arctic and Antarctic oceans. The last components of the expedition were slotting into place.

One fine morning Gino drove down to Portsmouth to try out a pair of Gypsy Moth seaplanes, taking with him two pilots from the Air Corps who had volunteered to join the expedition. They carried their leather flying helmets crammed into the pockets of their sports jackets. Gino as always was inappropriately but immaculately dressed in a suit.

The two DH60s with the new 135 HP engine were the latest off the de Havilland production line; the factory at Stag Lane, Edgeware was turning them out at a rate of one per day. The basic Moth had proved itself over the last five years. It was a light two-seater biplane of great versatility and toughness which could withstand rough usage, a Model T of the air. Built of canvas stretched on a wooden frame, the aircraft had a wingspan of 30 feet. The two flyers sat in tandem, with a 15-gallon fuel tank behind them. Fitted with floats as a seaplane, the DH60 had a maximum speed of 98mph, an operating ceiling of 13,000 feet, and a range of 300 miles.

After inspecting the aircraft on their moorings, the professional pilots had first go. Then Gino installed himself in the flying seat, turned it into the wind and gunned the motor, accelerating over rippled water that felt as hard as cobbles beneath the drumming floats. Completing a circuit he landed, taxied to the jetty and bought both planes on the spot. Then he raced back to London to change into evening dress, took Pam, Tony and Scott to see Noel Coward's *Bitter Sweet,* then went on to a dance. It was a good day.

The expedition's food and stores, some paid for but most cadged from the manufacturers, were sent direct to St Katherine's Dock. Before the *Quest* arrived from Norway these had to be checked, sorted and repacked into sledging boxes, each containing one week's rations for two men. At Onslow Crescent, Nanny and Cook were sewing food bags, knitting gloves and sweaters and making duffel slippers, assisted intermittently by Pam who, like Gino, was leading a busy social life. He accepted every invitation that came in, taking her and Tony with him whenever possible. He had become *de facto* head of this near-penniless family and felt some guilt about leaving them; he wanted everyone to enjoy the best time possible before his departure. He ended almost every evening at a dance, or rather with a tour of several dances. Then he would run home, still wearing dancing pumps, white tie and tails, through early-morning Mayfair and a Belgravia empty of traffic except for horse-drawn watercarts hosing down the streets. This was his rather quaint notion of 'training', and his only physical preparation for the rigours of the ice cap which awaited him.

Arriving from Norway, the *Quest* sailed up the Thames into St Katherine's Dock on 4 July. From then on her charter cost £20 per day. Money mattered, and she was loaded at high speed. The evening before the expedition sailed, Pam – at Gino's suggestion – threw a cocktail party on board the ship, which was followed by a dance given by Mr and Mrs Stephen Courtauld. The ship and the occasion provided a novel venue for a party at a time of parties. There were a great many guests, among them Lord Thomson, the Secretary of State for Air, and Sir Sefton Brancker, the Director of Civil Aviation, both of whom had shown a personal as well as a professional interest in the Air-Route Expedition, granting leave to the service pilots and mechanics who wished to join it. (Both men would lose their lives in the R101 airship disaster before the explorers returned to England.)

Stars come to the party too: George Robey, 'the prime minister of mirth', at the height of his music hall success and Elissa Landi, the film star whose current movie is aptly titled *Always Goodbye*. But despite the presence of these celebs, the press is not here. It has occurred to no one to publicise the expedition, and if it had they would have thought it bad form and a poor idea. Nothing has been announced, yet the largely unemployed residents of the neighbourhood have observed the preparations and now they can hear the sound of dance music. The docks are a deprived working area. There is little available by way of entertainment. A crowd has gathered around the gates onto the quay. The men are wearing flat caps with chokers knotted at the neck of collarless shirts, the women in shapeless skirts of drab cloth. Their children's clothes are patched and some are barefoot. Almost all here are on the dole (75p per week for a man and his wife, 25p for each child).

Now the crowd stirs. Here comes another motorcar filled with overdressed toffs. It pulls up at the gates and a uniformed chauffeur in leggings springs out to open the doors. The occupants step out. Women in party frocks draw their skirts around them as they pick their way in satin shoes across the oily cobbles between casks and packing cases toward the brightly lit ship, as another car draws up to disgorge its load of guests. The crowd looks on... and the contrast between these two tribes of people is so stark you watch for signs of resentment in the mob; you await a mocking jeer or catcall, and it is surely reasonable to expect one... but it does not come. Why not, you wonder? There have been previous demonstrations against the 'ruling class', as these partygoers are perceived to be. Yet, as still another car arrives, instead of hissing or resentful silence a cheer goes up. The crowd claps and calls out in encouragement and approval. The lives of the men and women watching are wretched; witnessing the arrival of these to-be-envied guests how is it their reaction is applause? Why? Is it perhaps because they know the *reason* for this party, and the departure of the *Quest* has touched a chord within them, played upon some nerve deep in the unconscious of the group-mind? An airplane – the very symbol of the future – is lashed down on deck. This ship's young explorers are sailing, flying, into the white unknown in an attempt to open up the world. The idea connects to myth. The crowd's present is dire indeed but their imagination is free and will travel with them.

The *Quest* has been transformed. The ship's rigging is gay with bunting streamers and coloured fairy lights, her decks have been scrubbed and polished, a band is playing and Captain Schjelderup has put on his bowler hat in honour of the occasion. The deck, piled with crates, stores, equipment, is jammed with a throng of people. An ardent all-male court is gathered around Elissa Landi, others surround George Robey, laughing at his lines. The older generation of parents and senior officers are assembled in the stern, a steward moves between them topping up their glasses with champagne. Amidship, the Norwegian sailors and some of the explorers and their friends are getting rather out of hand, singing boisterously and dancing, and a couple have climbed the mast. This is the first time all the members of the expedition (except Scott, who was to meet them in the Faroes with the sledge dogs) are together, aboard ship on the eve of departure. Elated, fit and carefree, they are high on joy.

The hubbub, lights and music make an incongruous scene in the dank, river-smelling darkness of the docks. Work here has been slack for years, but it so happens that this evening another ship lies moored at the adjacent quay. A research vessel of the old tradition is fitting out for a long Antarctic voyage. Her crew is made up of older men and none of them are singing or dancing or climbing the mast. They, like the young explorers, are drinking, but they do so in silence, out of sight below deck. They too are about to sail for the polar regions but – unlike these youths – they know the zone where they are going. And they knew that to set sail for that place is not a reason to rejoice.

But on board the *Quest* the mood of the young explorers is carefree and exalted. Jazz is playing and their destination looks to them a winter playground. Tomorrow they are off on an adventure.

THE *QUEST*

THE *QUEST* SAILED on Sunday morning, July 6. She was a sturdy wooden ship of 125 tons, 111 feet in length, with bows strengthened to resist the ice. Originally built as a sealing vessel, in 1921 she had been bought by Sir Ernest Shackleton for his last expedition – he died aboard her in the Antarctic. Sold to a Norwegian sealing company, in 1928 she had played a prominent role in the search for General Nobile and his crew after the airship *Italia* crashed on the frozen Polar Ocean in an attempt to overfly the North Pole. The ship had already proved herself in the Arctic – unlike all but two of her crew that Sunday morning.

Her rigging bright with bunting and flying the Air-Route Expedition's flag, a polar bear with wings, the *Quest* steamed slowly down the Thames saluted by a cacophony of ships' sirens hooting farewell to the explorers at their departure for the Arctic. Shortly before one o'clock they stopped for luncheon. Stephen Courtauld's yacht *Virginia* was waiting for them, hove to off Gravesend, and they transferred aboard her for a final party.

It was here Gino said goodbye to Pam and Tony. No one said anything special; he might have been off on a skiing holiday and expected home in a week. True to the British tradition, the chatter of the other guests was similarly undisturbed by any show of emotion until, with a yell of agony and spray of blood, all hell broke loose in the saloon. Their host's pet lemur, whose signs of discontent had gone unnoticed by the lunch party, had launched itself in a frenzied attack on Captain Lemon, the expedition's signals officer, on loan from the Army. The enraged beast had clamped its jaw on his hand, severing an artery. Blood flew everywhere, splattering the guests, and chaos erupted. Moments later the creature had been pried loose and order was restored. Coffee was served while Surgeon-Lieutenant Bingham (lent by the Navy) staunched the wound but was seen to be rather inexpert in sewing it up. The explorers eventually returned to the *Quest* and, blooded by their first casualty, sailed onward for the north.

Scott was waiting for them in the Faroe Islands with the sledge dogs he had bought in west Greenland. On board the expedition party numbered thirteen. Their average age was twenty-five, eighteen months more than that of their leader. Under Stephenson, the chief surveyor, came Chapman, Courtauld, Rymill and Lindsay, all of whom had completed a crash course in mapping given by the map curator of the RGS. Lawrence Wager, an experienced mountaineer, was the geologist of the group, Quintin Riley the meteorologist. Then there were the pilots who would fly the two De Havilland Gypsy Moths (one of which, deconstructed and covered in tarpaulin, was lashed down among the crates and equipment on the *Quest*'s deck): Flight-Lieutenant D'Aeth came from the Air Corps; Iliffe Cozens was the second pilot. Rymill, Courtauld and Gino held flying licences and could act as back-up pilots as necessary. The aircraft engineer, Hampton, came from the Reserve. Captain Lemon, the signals officer, and Bingham, the surgeon, completed the company.

The *Quest* was overloaded with men and cargo. Gino had the small cabin which Shackleton had occupied on his last voyage, but he shared it with two others. Some slept in the saloon, the rest were crowded into cabins and deck houses. The Norwegian crew slept in the unventilated hold, whose timbers were impregnated with seal blood, in conditions of such noxious barbarity the gorge rises at the attempt to imagine them. There was nowhere to sit on deck, no bath aboard or even a basin with running water. In these cramped and uncomfortable quarters the members of the expedition got to know each other – and their leader. Breakfast was at half-past nine. Gino said he hoped this was not too early for anyone.

The President of the Royal Geographical Society would write later of Gino that, 'he was destined to command… leadership came to him naturally.' Maybe, but he had showed little evidence of it as a child, rather the contrary. At the age of nine he had been sent as a boarder to prep school where he failed to distinguish himself at work and took no interest in sport. 'His quiet and unassuming character,' his headmaster wrote later, 'gave no hint whatsoever of the force of his character. We who knew him intimately never guessed how his childish characteristics would develop.' To this Scott added: 'The interesting thing is that to all appearances they never did, a fact which made what he achieved appear still more remarkable.'

Immediately after the end of World War I in 1918, Gino went to France to spend the school holidays with Colonel Watkins who was on the staff of XIII Corps. For a boy of eleven it was a remarkable experience. At Corps' headquarters in the devastated area around Cambrai he and his father shared a billet whose roof had been blown to pieces, a deficiency which much distressed their batman who had been second footman to a peer. Neatly dressed in shorts, Gino dined in the mess among a dozen staff officers, entirely at ease in their company. He passed his days accompanying his father on his duties or with one of the military salvage parties in the field helping with their work, to return in the evening happy and tired, covered in mud and still wearing his pink school cap. He wrote to his grandmother: 'I am out here with Daddy and having a very nice time. There are not any houses standing in the village here. I have seen a lot of broken-up towns. There were a great many bombs and bullets and helmets and machine-gun bands lying about. We went to look at the cemetery here yesterday. It is a very big one. Daddy sends you his best love and says I am quite a nice boy.'

When he was thirteen Gino applied to join the Royal Navy as a midshipman (as had his Uncle Bobby who rose to become First Lord). Though he passed the interview, he failed the examination and was rejected. He was disappointed, but for someone who detested authority as much as Gino did the Navy would surely have proved disastrous.

Arctic explorers are a singular brand of people. Not everyone is drawn to quit the comforts of our world to spend months or years subsisting on filthy food, cold, celibate and often in danger, isolated on the frozen summit of the globe. What these men do is abnormal and masochistic. When reading of their exploits the question is insistent: *why on earth should they wish to do it?*

Perhaps the answer can be found in their schooling, the manner in which they were raised as children of the tribe. Gino's name had been put down for his father's school, Eton, at birth, but had been removed when he entered for the Navy. There was no place for him; instead he was sent to Lancing. He entered the school for the spring term of 1920. It was the start of a tribal rite of passage, the same five-year conditioning process imposed upon Scott, Courtauld, Chapman and other members of the later Air-

Route Expedition, to which youths of their sort traditionally had been subjected for the last several hundred years. All were shaped by – or in reaction to – the Public School system. By the twenties this was represented by a number of schools, differing in their fees and social standing but fairly consistent in what and how they taught. Their purpose was to prepare a youth to administer his country and empire. This education may be described as privileged, but it did not feel *advantaged*; quite deliberately the contrary.

Within the system an academic education was available but this was not its only significant component. Indeed, in the order of priorities listed by the famous Dr Arnold in *Tom Brown's Schooldays*, academic ability ranked third after the induction of religion and moral principle and the correct conduct of an English gentleman. What these institutions aimed to teach was a vocation to govern and administer, and to do so justly as well as expediently. It was an ethos founded on the five cardinal virtues recognised in the ancient world as the basis of enlightened behaviour: courage, wisdom, justice, piety and moderation. And from the same classical sources came the importance accorded to physical fitness, to games and competitive sport. Winning was good, both on the sports field and (less so) in scholarship. Success was applauded and rewarded with celebrity, but to *exult* in success was deplored. Discipline and self-control were seen as all-important, as was obedience without servility. Conformity and integrity were necessary, together with an acceptance of brutality; perhaps fostering this acceptance was the point of the infamous 'fagging' system. Never complain, however gross the reason to do so.

Lancing school stood in an isolated position on the South Downs, far from shops or other community, facing down the bare slopes of the hills to a desolate gravel shore which nowhere but in Britain would be called a 'beach'. Resembling a medieval monastery in its cheerless appearance, the cluster of flintstone buildings was dominated by the imposing chapel which jutted from the hillside like the prow of a ship in monumental affirmation to the Anglican faith. The school was divided into seven Houses, each holding 50–60 boys, containing dormitories, and studies for the most senior. The communal House Room was large, with an empty fireplace, illuminated by gaslight and furnished with long tables and wooden benches. One wall was lined by lockers, one for each student, his only private space. A tall, glass-fronted cabinet exhibited silver cups and sporting trophies won by the House. Beside this shrine a notice board displayed edicts, appointments, ordinances and secular texts. The House tutors all were bachelors and no woman's hand or trace of domesticity had been permitted to soften the austerity of the setting.

Meals were taken in School Hall with the various Houses ranged at their own tables and the masters seated on a raised dais but eating the same ill-cooked food prepared from the cheapest ingredients available: a thin stew of boiled vegetables with floating scraps of gristle, sausages of compressed greasy offal, potatoes with maggots, honey-sugar (a sweetened, cheesy mush served in a cardboard tub), cocoa, margarine, unlimited white bread. The diet was not only disgusting but inadequate and nutritionally deficient. Boys spent their pocket money – usually one shilling per week – in the Grub Shop which sold cream cakes, ices, pastries, chocolate and sweets. Sunday teas, which were privately organised, constituted the high point of the week. In their own secluded room the House Captains were served by fags with delicacies such as foie gras and Gentleman's Relish purchased before the start of term at Fortnum & Mason or Harrods. The boys with private studies entertained friends to carefully planned meals of only slightly lesser quality. In the House Room the underprivileged wolfed their stores crouched over their tuck boxes while their immediate superiors, the members of the Settle (the lowest stratum of authority) took it in turns trying to outdo each other through the size and scale of the feast they paid for and hosted. Evelyn Waugh, who was at Lancing during the same period as Gino, details these teas as beginning with crumpets, 'eight or more a head, dripping with butter. From there we swiftly passed to cake, pastry and, in season, strawberries and cream, until at six we tottered into chapel bloated and stupefied with eating.' As the reader may be aware, he remained fond of food until his death, aged 64, from drink, snobbery and constipation.

Unseen females worked in the kitchens, made the beds and cleaned the dormitories. Waugh also describes a tribe of illiterate and misshapen 'bootmen' who apparently lived in lightless tunnels beneath Great School, and smelled of blacking and shag. These unhappy men emerged morning and evening, trundling huge wheeled baskets of dirty or clean boots, muttering to themselves as they stumbled along with eyes fixed upon the ground.

Each House Room was run by the members of the Settle. Above them in the hierarchy came the prefects, and above these the House Captains. These two groups were served by 'fags', junior boys performing the initiatory duty imposed upon all. The House Captains had authority to administer corporal punishment, usually by three strokes of the cane. The House tutor and headmaster also flogged their pupils who were bent over a chair to receive four or six strokes across the buttocks. Although not displayed in the House Room's glass-fronted shrine with other cult and fetishist images, the cane was an all-powerful totem. Its practice – receiving it when young, administering it as a senior – was fundamental to the culture.

Compulsory outdoor games took place every afternoon, whatever the weather: rugby, cricket, running, boxing, swimming. These were intensely competitive; to achieve the House team was to be acknowledged, to become someone. At matches everybody turned out to support the House. Following the afternoon's sport, players shared the same two tubs of tepid, muddy water. One clean towel was issued per week. Boys attended chapel every morning and evening, and three times on Sunday. Hymns were rousing and loudly sung. Lengthy sermons inculcated muscular Christian principles and their judicious application to worldly life.

From the day he entered the school to the date he left, each boy was governed by a rigid set of rules, taboos, ceremonies and incantations. House prayers had to be learnt by heart; a new 'man' (aged thirteen) had to recite them before an invigilating prefect to prove himself word-perfect in the rubric. On the third Sunday of his first term he was put through an initiation when, standing on the Settle table, he had to sing a song to the assembled House. From then on he was a full member of the tribe, subject to fagging and beating and expected to look after himself.

The day was spent in classrooms, on the playing fields and in the House, but after breakfast boys congregated at the Groves. Here they socialised and gossiped with members of other Houses while performing the essential ceremony of the morning. The Groves was a whitewashed yard of urinals and latrines without doors built over an open sewer only occasionally sluiced clean. These exposed privies were inadequate in number; you had to bag your turn and hang around in this English version of the Greek *stoa*.

Sex – or, more exactly, repressed sexuality – pulsed in an electric undercurrent beneath the day's routine. Some masters selected favourites from among their brighter and better-looking students, while between the boys seductions, love affairs and betrayals played out their mostly unconsummated course. Masturbation was considered weakening to the physique and moral fibre, and proscribed. Sex was regarded as 'filth'. The boys had been given biological information on the reproductive act but very few had seen a photograph of a naked woman. Male on male activity was

Gino with his mother. One morning she kissed her children goodbye and caught a train to Eastbourne. At the station she hired a taxi to Beachy Head. Paying off the cab, she walked to the cliff's edge and jumped. Her body was never found.

Colonel Watkins. Family life did not appeal to him. Fecklessness and an infallible eye for a dud investment soon lost him all he'd inherited, but it did not restrict his travelling. From Moscow he brought back two wild bears as presents for his children. Installed at Eaton Place, they failed to become the cuddly pets he envisaged.

The Watkins Family. *Gino's grandmother is on the left, to whom all bills were sent for settlement. Pam, Tony and Gino surround their father; their mother stands on the right. At the start of one school term there was no money for rail fares and the children had to hide from the ticket collector in the train's lavatory.*

Dumbleton Hall. *The home of Uncle Bobby, where they spent their holidays in unaccustomed luxury.*

Training in Chamonix. *Gino's rather quaint idea of training for the rigours of the ice cap the winter before the expedition sailed for the Arctic. Note tie.*

Gino aged 18. *Clinging to a cliff by your fingernails above a sheer drop of vertical rockface is not most people's idea of fun, yet for him it was an epiphany which can be compared to the stirring of religious faith or the first taste of a drug.*

The Roaring Twenties. *The Jazz Age belonged to the young. The Blackbirds Negro Revue arrived from America, bringing with it the charleston and Josephine Baker. For the young explorers preparing for the Arctic, there was a lot of living to be fitted in.*

The Gypsy Moth seaplane. *Gino poses on one of the Gypsy Moth seaplanes with the two expedition pilots. The two aircraft cost £3,200 – a quarter of the expedition's budget.*

The Moth's cockpit. *The DH60 Moth with the new 135 HP engine was a two-seater biplane of proven toughness which could stand rough usage; a sort of Model T of the air.*

What a chap wears to the Arctic. *The departure of the* Quest *at the start of the expedition. Seeing them off, on the left, is Vilhjalmar Stefansson, who believed a man could live indefinitely in the Arctic without any commodity from the civilized world except matches. (He did so himself for five years.)*

The Quest. *Navigating through pack ice to the Greenland coast.*

'They'd dressed up to welcome us...'
The arrival of fourteen young Englishmen in
sports jackets, ties and Oxford bags was the
most astounding experience the Eskimos had
ever known. The explorers first action was to
set a wind-up gramophone on the rocks and
teach them to dance the charleston.

The base hut. *The hut accommodated fourteen explorers plus three Eskimo girls in the loft.*

Lunch in the base hut. *Gino and Chapman are on the right. 'Everything was beautifully clean and in it's right place, and the Eskimo staff equally immaculate. They did all the cleaning, laid the table, washed up and brought the dishes round to the left side as if they'd been used to it all their lives.'*

not acknowledged as existing. Such filth was unmentionable, worse even than filth with women. A few years later when this same intake of youths were at university, Evelyn Waugh estimated that fewer than 10 per cent of them had heterosexual experience.

In his last term before leaving Lancing to go to Oxford, Waugh wrote an editorial in the school magazine analysing the generation which he and Gino (and the members of the Air-Route Expedition) shared.

What will the young men of 1922 be? They will be, above all things, clear-sighted, they will have no use for phrases or shadows... And because they are clear-sighted, they will not be revolutionaries... there will be much that they will lose, but all they have will be real. And they will be reticent... middle-aged observers will find it hard to see their soul. But they will have – and this is their justification – a very full sense of humour... They will watch themselves with, probably, a greater egotism than did the young men of the 'Nineties, but it will be with a cynical smile and often with a laugh. It is a queer world which the old men have left them and they will have few ideals and illusions to console them... They will not be a happy generation.

After finishing this book about Gino and the party of young men he led to the Arctic, the reader may be interested – if he or she remembers – to refer back to Waugh's prognosis.

The aim of the system endured by that group, now on board the *Quest* on her passage north, was to standardise attitudes and inculcate 'good form'. It taught the virtues that it believed went towards a civilised life. The price the system demanded was conformity. It stifled self-expression and independent thinking.

Gino fitted in with the regimen not at all. He showed little academic promise and detested organised games, seeing no point in them. The only activity he excelled in was the lonely sport of cross-country running. He also became a crack shot with both rifle and revolver, representing Lancing at Bisley where he scored higher than any other competitor.

He was instinctively an excellent climber. 'Some of the things he did were almost too spectacular to watch,' says a school friend. 'I remember on one occasion he climbed round the Masters Tower, an incredibly difficult business; I have never heard of anyone else who tried it.' As to work, he did not trouble himself with it. 'We used to spend our time laughing at each other, laughing at the absurdities of our various subjects and of those who taught us, always magnifying the slightest chance of a joke.' It was the affectation of Gino's clique, then and later, that they took nothing seriously, a pose which he himself never quite shook off.

On the long vacation from Cambridge, Gino spent the whole summer at Chamonix, climbing the Alpine peaks with a guide. Climbers are more often met with than explorers, but again this is an activity not many are drawn to. Clinging to a cliff by your fingernails above a sheer drop of vertical rock-face is not most people's idea of fun. Yet for Gino that summer was an epiphany. The seed of a desire took root in him which can be compared to the stirring of religious faith, or to the first taste of a drug which will become the user's ruling passion. On returning to Cambridge he signed up for a course of lectures on 'Man in the Polar Regions' given by Raymond Priestley, a don who had been in the Antarctic with Captain Scott and Shackleton. While walking back to his rooms with fellow undergraduate Quintin Riley after one of these talks, he remarked, 'I think we'd better go to the Arctic, Quintin.'

He sought out J. M. Wordie, a tutor at St John's who had been with Shackleton for three years in the Antarctic, first trapped in a sinking ship, then together with twenty-six others drifting on the ice in appalling discomfort and danger, until they found themselves marooned on Elephant Island for over four months before finally being rescued. Wordie was planning an expedition to the Arctic for that summer, but this team was already complete. Gino's response was original but characteristic. If he couldn't go with Wordie he would lead an expedition there himself. It was a presumptuous notion; others may have questioned his ability but Gino never doubted it himself. Scott details the skills which qualified him to lead such an expedition and these have an endearing quaintness to the modern reader. Gino was well read on the Arctic, a good climber and a competent skier; 'Above all the years he had spent in leading a varied life at a minimum expense (while at Cambridge he never spent more than the £400 yearly allowance with which he paid all his college and vacation bills) had taught him how to use money and how to adapt himself to any circumstance.' *To the Arctic?* The idea causes one to blink.

As his destination for that first expedition Gino chose Edge Island, an uninhabited area of mountain wilderness 500 miles north of Norway. The 2,500 square miles of interior was unexplored and the only sketch of the island's outline – much of this indicated only by dotted lines – dated from a Russo-Swedish expedition of 1899. Assembling a party of surveyors, geologists and mountaineers (eight in all, two of them twice his own age), he sailed for the island, crossing the Arctic Circle on Bastille Day, July 14. To celebrate his entry to the Polar regions, Gino took a dip. A swift plunge into the freezing water between the ice-floes christened him in his revealed vocation: explorer. He was nineteen years old.

Aboard the *Quest* and once again heading for the Arctic, Gino is twenty-two and the leader of a party of fourteen men. The *Quest* is a broad-beamed tubby little ship, decks stacked with gear, and her fresh paintwork shows very white on the grey water in contrast to the coal-grimed river traffic. Smoke from her funnel is snatched away by the breeze, small waves slap against the bows. Above the thump of her engine you can hear jazz music from a gramophone playing in the saloon. Coming out of the Thames estuary the vessel begins to roll a little in the cross-swell as she turns north. The steel needle skids screeching across the vinyl and the gramophone has to be stowed away.

The party of explorers pass their time in the saloon, where they eat, lounge about, smoke and talk. The air in the crowded space is thick with tobacco fumes; Gino is the only non-smoker. The role he plays is not that of leader but of host. At every meal he clambers over the others' backs to take his place seated on a heap of bedding at the head of the table. A member of the group, writing afterward, explains:

> The object... was to amuse, to shock if possible. All adjectives were exaggerated, all stories were outrageous and, above all, nothing was serious. There were no rules of conduct. The result, intentional or not, was that everyone became acquainted to the extent that they felt completely at ease in each other's company and yet knew nothing at all about their private lives. We were not shipmates; we were chaps or something of that sort. One cannot write exactly what we were...

All except Gino were known by their surnames.

One evening the conversation was dominated by a discussion about people's motives for going rock climbing. Courtauld started it. He had been talking about the ascent of Petermann Peak in northeast Greenland and mentioned that he had been quite content to stop a hundred feet or so below the summit because he had already been able to do all the necessary surveying. Such a point of view was almost blasphemous to the few serious mountaineers who heard him, and who themselves would have given a good deal to climb what was then believed to be the highest mountain in the Arctic. Wager, the geologist, said that he scarcely noticed the type of rock he climbed on so long as it did not break or crumble: he enjoyed fulfilling an objective, and if he had to struggle against bad weather the fight was still more worthwhile. Chapman, the most reckless and idealistic climber of the lot, was in search of mental and physical justification by striving against all the difficulties he could find and overcoming them. Then, made worthy by achievement, he could stand upon the summit and admire the glorious view. But Gino did not at once admit that desire for achievement had anything to do with his love of climbing. When challenged to reveal his motivation he confessed that *it was the thrill of being frightened that he most enjoyed.*

It is a remarkable admission. His listeners were men he was leading on an expedition into unexplored territory of unknown conditions, containing unknown perils. They had entrusted their lives into his hands. No one took up on Gino's disclosure, nor did they discuss it later among themselves. At the start of the expedition it would have been unthinkable to question the suitability of their leader. But for some, reflecting on it privately, it must have been a little disquieting to learn that his underlying reason for taking them to the Arctic lay in his taste for *the adrenalin rush of danger.*

Dancing the Charleston

on Ice

Right from the start the standards of civilisation began to shred and fall away. There was no bathroom in the *Quest* and the only way for a man to shave or wash was in a bucket on deck with a bar of seawater soap. In Blythe the ship stopped to fill up with coal. Its gritty dust blew everywhere, getting into the explorers' bedding, lodging in the creases of their clothes, sticking to their skin. The weather worsened as they sailed up the coat of Scotland, the sky grew overcast. The *Quest* pitched in the waves and the new ropes securing the airplane and the cargo creaked alarmingly as they took the strain. It started to drizzle, and those on deck felt the slash of cold salt spray. They crowded into the saloon or lay queasily trying to read in their cramped quarters.

There was a loud shout from on deck, 'Come up!' They scrambled up the companionway. On the bridge the captain was leaned out, jabbing excitedly at the sky. They looked up, and saw a phantasm emerging from the murk, the swollen shape of a huge silver airship buffeting against the wind only 200 feet above as the *Graf Zeppelin* passed slowly overhead, battling her way through the scudding clouds back to Germany at the end of her voyage around the world. They watched in silence, gripping the rigging for support as the deck heaved beneath them – and even the seasick among them briefly forgot their suffering for this was a symbolic moment: a sight of the enemy. Their purpose in the Arctic was to open up a route for fixed-wing planes and put that airship and all the others out of business.

The sea continued rough as they sailed north. Many of them were sick, including Gino. It did not stop the rest from smoking. Only Surgeon-Lieutenant Bingham had any work to do, when the ship's carpenter thrust his fist into the metal propeller of the wind generator the meteorologists had rigged up on the bridge. Apparently he wanted to see what would happen. And the grotesque motif initiated when Captain Lemon was mauled by a lemur over lunch was repeated when the *Quest's* captain used an axe to behead a live turkey. The wings of the headless bird began to flap furiously, and it scampered away across the deck splashing gore over captain and steward who had to capture and cling to it with all their strength to prevent it from escaping and flying away.

On July 12, the *Quest* reached the Faroe Islands and cruised the ragged coast searching for Captain Mikkelsen's whaling station where Scott was waiting with the sledge dogs he had bought in west Greenland. A boatload of fishermen guided them through the entrance to the narrow fjord. The ghastly reek of the place overwhelmed them even before they saw it. Then as they rounded the headland a mob of huskies raised their muzzles to the sky and began howling like a wolf pack. Freakish and elemental, the sound reached back to some ancestral memory in the listeners; heard for the first time it was chilling.

The *Quest* anchored off the whaling station as the small harbour was occupied by the carcasses of a finback and two killer whales attached to buoys. Hundreds of shrieking gulls flapped and fought and fed on the scum of bloody refuse floating on the water. The air was thick with the choking stench of rotting meat laced with fumes from the factory rendering whale blubber into oil. Scott came out in a boat to meet them. Wearing a thick sweater and coarse tweed jacket, one of his hands was wrapped in a dirty bandage and he stank abominably, but he told Gino and the others that he had forty-nine sledge dogs and a ton of raw whale meat and blubber to feed both beasts and men over the weeks to come. This was his contribution to the party, but the information delivered amid the foul odour of putrefying offal was not received as the good news Scott imagined it to be. Nevertheless, alone in west Greenland with limited money, he had done well to buy and ship so many dogs, losing only one which had killed nine sheep before it could be shot. He had fulfilled his mission ably.

With great uproar, difficulty and danger the savage dogs were transferred to a wire pen constructed amidships on the *Quest's* deck, which was now so obstructed by crates, airplane and animals it could not be walked but had to be squeezed through like a maze. Scott's whale meat was taken on board. Some of this was already dried, but most had been recently cut from the carcasses in the harbour. These strips of raw and bloody flesh the queasy explorers hung in the ship's rigging so they might dry.

The whaling station was a repulsive, nauseating experience and they sailed on with relief – into bad weather. The *Quest* was round-bottomed, as ice-ships must be to ride up when caught and squeezed. There's an axiom: 'The better the ice-ship the worse she is in weather.' The *Quest* was an excellent ice-ship and she rolled to 40° with her decks awash from bow to stern. Nothing affected the huskies' appetites but most of the explorers were sick as dogs. Scott's damaged hand was examined by Surgeon-Lieutenant Bingham. He had taken a deep bite in the base of the thumb and the hand was swollen and infected. The surgeon cleaned and redressed the wound but it was clear Scott was in some pain. 'Sleep in my bunk,' Gino suggested, insisting that he himself could sleep equally well upon the floor. A graceful gesture says Scott, who was glad to accept.

The two men had first met two years previously, for Scott's tutor at Cambridge was Raymond Priestley. 'Several undergraduates were sitting in his rooms,' Scott writes, 'Smoking and listening to some of the polar stories which were not included in his lectures, and I said that I should like to travel about a bit before settling down to a job. Priestley said, "Watkins is planning to go to Labrador, you had better go and see him."' He went to Trinity next day. 'I found the door with H. G. Watkins painted above it. I knocked and was told to come in; then apologised and prepared to withdraw.' Of the two figures in the room one was dressed only in a wet towel tied around his waist. The other, a frail elegant young man wearing a roll neck sweater and white knickerbockers lounged in a chair with legs extended and the heels of his two-tone shoes resting on a desk. Scott writes:

I felt certain that I was in the wrong room. But the man in the armchair sprang up and called me back with "I'm Watkins, are you Scott?" The man in the bath towel disappeared and we began to talk. On a map Watkins showed me the journeys he proposed to make in Labrador. He talked about the country as if he could see it while he spoke... A few surveying parties had followed the main rivers by canoe... but the rest was unknown except from the reports of trappers and Indians. I had come to Watkins' room in a spirit of vague curiosity: I walked home half an hour later with nothing in my mind except Labrador and him. The smooth course of my life had been changed by the youth I had been talking to. He came to tea with me the next week and said that he could definitely take me with him: so would I mind learning all I could about photography, geology and botany?

Scott was both dazzled and shocked by Gino. In dress and manner he was not at all the sort of man he cared for, indeed he was quite hostile to the type; Gino looked like a 'queer'. Yet when he spoke of exploration and the Arctic he changed into another man. As he talked of it, that far wilderness became visible and real for Scott; his words touched those same nerves in him that had thrilled to the exploits of Amundsen and Shackleton when he was a boy. And so it was that from an effete young man in two-tone shoes Scott came to hear the call of the north. Gino had something he did not possess himself, a style, grace, flair which formed no part of his own nature; some element of air where Scott's was earth. Along with that, Scott already knew of Gino's reputation as a mountaineer who had led an expedition to Edge Island; despite his appearance, Gino was a man of action. Scott was hooked, but not just on the idea of an adventure. There was another factor, and one name for it is hero-worship.

After leaving the Faroe Islands it took the *Quest* two days, pitching through heavy weather, to reach Iceland. It was only when the explorers rose from their bunks and palely came ashore at Reykjavik to enjoy hot baths and dinner at the splendid new hotel that they noticed that their entire supply of whale blubber tied to the ship's rigging had shaken free in the storm and disappeared. Three months food rations of nauseating fat had gone over the side. It was a joyous moment. 'Everyone was in good spirits and no wonder,' Gino noted in his diary. 'The dinner cost 400 kroner of which 300 was for drink.' Taking on more coal at this last opportunity to fill up, the *Quest* sailed on next morning. The weather improved, and two days later whales were spouting in calm seas all round the ship. Just before sunset that night some of the party on deck thought they could glimpse a band of brightness glimmering on the horizon. Ice-blink, that pulse in the sky that signals the presence of ice.

Thump! They're almost thrown from their bunks by the thud of impact which jolts through all the timbers of the vessel. *Clang, clang, clang,* the brassy jangling of the ship's bell has them scrambling for their clothes. They rush on deck and, emerging from the gloom below, the light is so intense it blinds them. They have to shield their eyes to look. They are in the pack-ice. In the slanting blaze of dawn the view ahead is a mosaic of glittering white ice broken up by intersecting leads of dark water. By the ship the sea is clear as glass and the green-blue tints of submerged ice slither and meld below the surface in liquid colour. Fat black seals lie on the ice floes, basking in the sun. A quarter-mile away a light show is taking place where a gigantic iceberg looms and sparkles behind a diaphanous curtain of diffusing mist. In the far distance the white wall of Greenland's coastal mountains rears up against a pale peach and blue sky, the tall spikes of its icy peaks twined by thin streamers of inky cloud. Shading their eyes in the glare of silver light, the explorers gaze at a primordial landscape, vast and purely white yet dancing and glittering with flares of colour, as of jewels in the sun in the stillness of eternal day. They do not speak as they stare at the scene. Awe has stunned them, they are silenced by the spectacle of the sublime.

It takes three more days of slow going to reach the coast. As they approach it, the pack ice becomes thicker. The ship has to force its way through the close-jammed floes. Sometimes they are halted for an hour or more till the pattern changes in the current and the captain – who had been joined by Gino in the crow's nest – can identify a lead and call down his instructions to proceed. At these stops the explorers scramble down onto the floes to take some exercise. It is hot in the sun, they remove their shirts. Scott has brought several walrus-hide dog whips from West Greenland; short-handled, their plaited lash is five yards in length. They practise with them unsuccessfully, hurting others and themselves, cursing and laughing as they do so. By sunset on the third day they are through the pack. The *Quest* anchors off the coast and the captain sets out in the ship's boat to search for Eskimos to guide them through the ice-crammed channels of the archipelago into Angmagssalik. Next morning when the explorers come on deck it is into a jabber of excited noise. The water around the ship is thronged with Eskimo boats; the men in their single seater hunting kayaks, the women crowded into umiaks, the ungainly sealskin barges which forms the family transport. The sleek kayaks race ahead on the calm sea, 'paddled along furiously by little men in white sealskin jackets and white hats' who are so charged up by excitement that every now and then one of them flings his harpoon with tremendous force in front of him, scooping it up again with one hand as he races past in the water. These darting craft skimming the surface lead the way through the ice floes and the *Quest* steams slowly after, while the ranks of women in the umiaks paddle frantically to keep up, laughing and chattering and calling out like children as the incongruous fleet winds through the islands to anchor at Angmagssalik's jetty.

There is a bareness in the view: a rocky fjord beset by ice, no greenery, no trees, an elemental starkness. The larger of the only two settlements on the eastern seaboard of Greenland, the colony consists of about 700 Eskimos dispersed along the coast, a half-dozen wooden houses with red tin roofs, and two tall radio masts which blow down each winter. The European population numbers three and a half: a Danish magistrate/storekeeper, Danish wireless operator, his wife, and a mixed-race Christian missionary.

Eskimos have sledged for miles and gathered from up and down the coast. The expedition has been anticipated for weeks as the Big Event. There is nothing else competing for their attention as

– apart from some curious sexual practices we will come to later
– there is nothing whatsoever by way of entertainment, recreation
or diversion available in this godforsaken place. But now a ship!
Strangers! Men! This is a sensational occasion. And the explorers
too are excited by their arrival, keen to land and meet the locals, but
there's a hitch. 'It was not until after lunch we were allowed to go
ashore,' one of them, Chapman, writes. 'There was quite a deal of
business to go through before.' He doesn't elaborate in his diary, but
there was indeed. Before they set sail for Greenland, Gino had to
lodge a financial bond with the Danish Government to indemnify
the administration against the cost of illegitimate births resulting
from the visit; now, each of the young explorers has to line up, drop
his trousers and expose his penis to detailed examination by the
magistrate to ensure he brings no venereal infection into this pure
land.

Then, buttoning up their flies, they go ashore to meet the
public. All they take with them from the ship are Gino's wind-
up gramophone and their collection of the latest dance records.
They set it up on a piece of flat land by the shore. Cranking it
up, Gino puts on Jack Buchanan. The Eskimos crowd round.
The men are small with lank dark hair, sepia-yellow faces and
bright enigmatic smiles. 'The women… are more interesting,'
Chapman notes. 'A few of them had put on skirts for our benefit
– unfortunately. I danced…' *Fancy our meeting / For just one fond
greeting / When days are so fleeting and few.* Explorers, ship's crew
and Eskimo girls all dance: a frenzied, double-beat jigging set by
the women in their red sealskin boots. Wearing bright blouses,
beads and ornamented seal-fur trousers, they have dressed up in
party gear and are as agitated as jumping beans with the thrill
of it all.

Angmagssalik is supplied by a once-a-year ship from Denmark;
it is remote and inaccessible as an outpost can be. Visitors are almost

unknown and the arrival of fourteen young Englishmen in sports jackets, ties and Oxford bags is the most astounding occurrence the inhabitants have experienced in a long time. And this band of tall, athletic young aliens seems friendly. And very keen on dancing, for they've been cooped up on a ship for the last three weeks and are brimming full of energy.

I can't give you anything but love baby... The scratchy music rings out on the chilly air; Cole Porter, Jerome Kern, Gershwin... As the numbers end and the records are lifted off the turntable they are now no longer being carefully replaced in their brown paper sleeves but piled carelessly on the rocks beside the gramophone. Foxtrot and cakewalk, black bottom or blues, the steps the dancers move to are all the same: that relentless jigging imposed by the Eskimo girls never lets up. The trampled turf dissolves beneath their exuberant feet while around the muddy dance floor Eskimo men stand silently and watch from expressionless black eyes. *Rabloona*, palefaces, are what they call these visitors from an alien world. But they also have another name for them: *amasintiit*, stealers of our women.

A pause... and Gino sorts through the disordered stack to select another record. As its first jaunty bars ring out the explorers take the cue. They regain control of the party and lead the dance. They initiate the steps and, watching them, the Eskimo women are struck still, bemused and immobilised by astonishment. One girl comes forward to imitate the moves, then another, and another; clumsy at first before they get it and kick their legs askew, giggling in excitement.

Let's misbehave / We're all alone / No chaperone / Let's misbehave... Wildly, exuberantly, explorers and Eskimo women dance the charleston while afternoon becomes evening yet it does not grow dark, for the sun does not set but orbits behind the rim of the purple-shadowed mass of the coastal mountains which hold back the ice cap, that place so dreaded by the Eskimos. *Let's misbehave...* The same number plays again and again while, unnoticed above the dancers, the pinnacles of the mountains are still twined by those same ribbons of menacing black cloud.

The Land that God gave Cain

Next morning, the *Quest* sailed on under clear skies to search for a place suitable to establish a base camp for the expedition. The site had to combine several characteristics. First, it must provide access to the ice cap, a route by which men and dogs with heavily loaded sledges could climb the several thousand feet of steep ascent to reach it. It must include a source of fresh water. There had to be a shelving beach so the seaplanes could be launched easily when weather was suitable for flying, but also a sheltered deep-water anchorage for the *Quest* to unload. The spot should be exposed south to benefit from what winter sunshine there was, and should not be shut in by mountains which might block the radio signals. There was one additional requirement: as this would be the explorers home for a year and more when they were not travelling on the ice cap, Gino wanted a place where the hunting was good so they could provide themselves and their dogs with fresh food.

On the second day of the search the *Quest* entered a deep fjord thirty miles west of Angmagssalik, cruised the length of it and dropped anchor by a fairly level promontory. The mountaineers went off to examine the approach to the ice cap via a glacier at the head of the fjord. D'Aeth, the chief pilot, with Hampton, the amateur mechanic who had just come down from Cambridge, looked for a suitable beach for their seaplanes, and Lemon for a good position for his radio masts. All came back satisfied. In a series of rowdy and dangerously chaotic boat trips Scott transferred his pack of forty-nine savage dogs onto an island in the fjord and marooned them there (boating out once a day to feed them), and the work of establishing the base began at once. Scott writes:

Greenland as we saw it then was a land of barren mountains which ran down steeply into the sea where floated icebergs, calved from the glaciers, and numerous small floes. Beneath a clear sky these dominant colours, black and blue and white, were strikingly contrasted. Here and there were little fertile valleys, a freshwater lake surrounded by cotton grass, saxifrages and a kind of buttercup; but more often any gap between the mountains was filled by a glacier, its surface cracked by the steep gradient into dangerous-looking crevasses. These glaciers were like frozen streams escaping from a vast reservoir of unmelted snow which by its own pressure had formed itself into ice, hundreds or even thousands of feet deep. This lifeless desert rose gradually inland until it met the sky in an unbroken line of white against the blue. The whole of Greenland is like that: its coastal mountains hold in the ice which here and there leaks through the valleys to reach the sea and, in the form of icebergs, to float away. Think of a plate with a crenellated rim having sugar constantly shaken over it. If you can imagine this plate as pear-shaped and about 1,500 miles long, and the sugar as snow which never melts but very gradually slips outwards, you can form a picture of the Greenland ice cap.

Gino divided the party into two twelve-hour shifts so the work of unloading could be continuous. First the planks and material for building the base hut where they would live had to be rowed the 200 yards from ship to shore, then carried up the steep slope to where the *Quest's* carpenter and mate were erecting the building. Then the wireless equipment, kitchen range, stove, stores and personal kit had to be humped up the same rough path. 'The worst part was unloading the coal,' says Chapman. The sacks were filled in the airless, badly lit hold, then hoisted to the deck and lowered into the whale-boats – a tricky job due to the ship's faulty winch. They were then rowed precariously to shore, the boats so low in the water there were only inches of freeboard. Then came the hardest labour when each sack was heaved onto a man's shoulders and he had to hump it over the slippery rocks beyond the reach of the tide. Coal, the bulk of the stores, the ration boxes and dog-pemmican boxes, were all stacked on the foreshore, as well as the tins of petrol, oil and paraffin. Gino shirked nothing himself. Scott says, 'One remembers him at the end of a day spent in transporting coal: his face black except for his lips and a thin circle round each eye, and crowned, when he removed his knotted cotton handkerchief, with smooth fair hair. He did not look at all like the creator of an expedition'.

This unremitting shift-work continued for two weeks while crowds of Eskimo women and girls arrived in umiaks to stare, fingering everything they could lay their hands on and picking through the discarded tins and rubbish for items of use to them. 'They are very friendly and do not smell very much,' Chapman noted, though another man remarks that, 'it was not for another two months we had any leisure to appreciate them and realise what delightful people they are.'

The weather remained sunny and the explorers laboured in their shirtsleeves. By the start of August the material and stores were off-loaded and the hut completed, flanked by two seventy-foot radio masts, which gave the base camp a professional aspect that pleased everyone. The hut, which was walled by double layers of matchboarding and windproof felt, consisted of a 20 x 12 foot room with tiers of bunks along each side. The room led into a small kitchen, beyond which lay the wireless and workroom and a tiny photographer's darkroom. Above this series of rooms was a loft where personal kit was stored, which – as the party's living arrangements developed – would later become staff accommodation.

Now the fourteen members of the exhibition moved into their new quarters and prepared for the mission they had come here to accomplish. Their home base might be primitive and short of mod cons but for their intended work they possessed the latest and best equipment available – cutting-edge technology.

Fritz Lang's film *Metropolis* had opened in 1926, graphically illustrating the force powering the revolution in lifestyle taking place in America and western Europe: the machine. The machine was the future. People believed that new synthetic materials, mass production and automation would improve the whole quality of life. The machine stood for speed and progress, even for democracy, for mechanisation would make consumer items available to all. Abolishing drudgery, it would afford leisure and dignity to everyone.

Fashion designers picked up on this bold if erroneous conviction, translating it into a 'machine aesthetic': chic dresses of shiny metallic finish, steel beads (Chanel), shoes of patent leather that reflected the gleam of highly polished metal. The trend developed a further motif. Close-fitting flying caps and leather aviator jackets became fashionable must-haves. Tied at the bare throat or pinned to a hat, women wore stiffened scarves shaped into big bows which resembled airplane propellers. Foremost of all machines was the airplane. The airplane was the supreme totem of the age. Symbolising speed, glamour, travel, it incarnated a popular fantasy. It would liberate men and women from the bonds of who and what they were. It would make them cosmopolites and free citizens of the modern world.

One of the deconstructed Gypsy Moths was still lashed down on the deck of the *Quest*. Before D'Aeth and Hampton could rig and launch it the ice had to be cleared from the small bay where they planned to build a hangar. Using pickaxes and dynamite they removed it – and nearly themselves along with it – when one of the crew, humping a box of detonators, dropped it on the rocks. Once cleared, they stretched ropes across the mouth of the bay to prevent ice drifting in with the wind. The seaplane's floats were assembled and painted on deck. Then the *Quest*'s dangerously unreliable winch was used to hoist and lower the body of the aircraft onto the floats. Due to unloading, the ship had listed heavily to starboard and it was hard to fit them evenly. Complete except for its wings, the aircraft was lowered onto the water just as a squall blew up and a large ice floe drifted toward them, threatening to crush it against the side of the ship. Hurriedly the plane was towed into the bay and moored to a floating barrel. When the wind dropped the double wings were ferried over, precariously balanced between two boats. The men crewing the boats stood up and, in a hair-raising demonstration of synchronised wobbling, hoisted the wings on upraised arms so they could be bolted onto the fuselage. To everyone's astonishment, and great alarm among the watching Eskimos, the motor roared to life on the first swing of the propeller. The aircraft was, to all appearances, ready to fly.

D'Aeth and Hampton made the first trial, completing a circuit of the fjord. Nothing fell off and they landed safely. Gino took

Hampton's seat in the rear cockpit and the seaplane accelerated down a lane of clear blue water between scattered floes to take off for Angmagssalik, where he wanted to seek first-hand knowledge from the Eskimos about the ice cap. He had yet to learn the reality of that place where he and his men intended to go.

On 9 August the four-masted sailing vessel *Gustav Holm* arrived from Denmark carrying the second airplane and the rest of the expedition's stores. In the pale predawn light, the tall ship ghosted up the fjord to drop anchor beside the *Quest* with a roar of chain. She was unloaded at once, for the two-month period during which it was possible to penetrate the ice pack was drawing to a close and the captain was anxious not to become trapped here until the following summer. Stores were ferried ashore in the *Quest*'s whaleboats and the second Gypsy Moth, still in its crate, towed round to the hangar bay. The *Gustav Holm* was gone within twenty-four hours.

In Angmagssalik, Gino quizzed Eskimos who passed their summers hunting seals and game in the fjords further to the north. About the voyage he was on the point of starting in the *Quest* in order to map the coastline and survey the mountains which lay behind it, he learned much. About the ice cap he gained almost no information. They never climbed onto it. It was an icy wilderness, a shifting land of blizzards with malignant ghosts shrieking in the wind. His intention not just to travel but *winter* there was incomprehensible to the Eskimos; they were horrified by the plan (translated by the mixed-race missionary) that he exposed to them.

If he felt dismay at their reaction, Gino did not show it to the others. On returning to base he and Scott made a number of low-level flights over the glacier leading up to the ice cap from the head of the fjord, to identify the hazards and plot a route. Then with Chapman they set off with dogs and two sledges to flag a course which avoided the visible dangers and led to the top. At first there was no snow. Sledges, gear, and supplies to make a food depot for the next party had to be humped on their backs up a steep slope of scree and naked rock. Only after climbing almost a thousand feet did they reach the glacier, a broad frozen river winding down from the mountains. Chapman put up the tent on the loose scree of its bank and made camp, while Gino and Scott hitched some of the dogs to a sledge and pressed on.

Enclosed by steep mountains the frozen river snaked up the valley in an uneven chute glazed with colour and spangled light. The surface was slippery, bottle-green ice. In places it was split by fissures, wide jagged cracks dropping sheer to the riverbed far below. But on this stretch of the glacier these crevasses were few and, clear of snow at this season, fully visible to the two men urging their dog teams up the slope. A few miles further and the frozen river changed, abruptly angling up at 40° in an irregular slant of glassy ice. Impossible to scale without an axe to cut steps and spiked crampons on their boots. Impossible for the dogs and sledges. Impossible to go further by this way – yet what other way was there? 'Bugger!' Scott said, staring at the obstacle. 'Buggery Bank,' said Gino – and so it became known by all of them. It would live up to its name.

Back at the camp beside the frozen river, Chapman was preparing the evening meal when he saw a swift dark shape racing down its shiny surface. 'Their speed was unbelievable... I had no idea a sledge could go so fast. Their dogs... were coming down the hill at full gallop. Both men were sitting on the sledge as it bounced and crashed over the hummocky ice, at any moment threatening to overturn, till with a final spurt it reached the camp.' Their faces flushed and lit up by the cold ride, Gino and Scott were laughing like schoolboys.

Short of moving the base, there was no other practicable

route onto the ice cap except by way of the glacier. During the following week a party of four men managed to scale Buggery Bank by winching up the loaded sledges and hauling up each dog individually on a rope. Flagging a route which avoided the crevasses, they reached the head of the glacier and penetrated the ice cap to establish a food and fuel depot which they named Big Flag before returning to base.

A few days later the *Quest* steamed as near as the captain dared to the foaming mouth of the yellow stream which connected the ice cap with the sea. Crew and explorers humped the last supplies up the rocky shore and onto the glacier. Then Scott and the four men who were to establish the weather station lashed their loads onto five sledges and with the usual turmoil harnessed their dogs. Saying goodbye to the others, they started on a 250-mile journey to the interior of the country by a means of transport of which only Scott had any previous experience.

Completing the arduous haul to the foot of Buggery Bank, they paused to look back. The glacier writhed down between the mountains to the black waters of the fjord; the jagged coastline spread out beneath them backed by the white sweep of the pack ice stretching to the horizon, glazed pink by the sun; points of fire sparkled from icebergs that rose like icy citadels from the frozen landscape, and small, cottony clouds streamed slowly westward in a pastel-blue sky. Far below them, and so tiny it looked like a toy, they saw the *Quest*, with its seaplane lashed on deck, steam from the base fjord and turn north, carrying Gino and the rest of the explorers up a scarcely charted coast on the start of their own adventure. 'It was all so fantastic that nothing seemed impossible,' said Scott.

Chapman, Courtauld and five other members of the expedition sailed with Gino on the *Quest*; only Lemon remained at the base camp to man the radio station.

The ship was crowded. Gino had engaged two Eskimos as coastal pilots and in return for their services had agreed to transport their families who, now at the end of summer, were returning to their winter houses in the scattered coastal settlements to the north. Much of the *Quest's* deck was taken up by the seaplane but the rest was a mass of umiaks, kayaks, sledges, dogs and bundled tents; an impromptu slum swarming with children and adults fingering and examining everything within reach.

The weather remained flawless. The *Quest* steamed on a flat blue sea through loose pack ice, passing huge icebergs which reared up out of the mosaic of the floating landscape, flaring in the sun. In the vast surrounding silence seagulls flapped squawking around the ship or settled on the ice floes in orderly crowds. Far off the explorers saw a whale spout; then the glistening backs of a pod of five surfaced together by the ship, all spouting at the same moment before plunging from sight in a sleek, linked roll so smooth they hardly disturbed the water.

For the first time since their arrival in the Arctic, Gino and the rest of the party had time to relax. He and Stephenson, the chief surveyor, studied the serrated coastline whose mountains reared up steeply from the shore, comparing it to the inaccurate map made in 1900. Chapman the ornithologist observed the sea birds and, with queasy fascination, the Eskimos on deck. 'They seemed to be very friendly and inordinately fond of tobacco. It rather took my breath away to see them knock the hot ashes out of their pipes into their mouths, and then chew them with evident gusto.'

The families consisted only of healthy adults with few children and those mostly boys – almost no old people. Their hard elemental lives centred around food and hunting. When old age or infirmity made you unproductive, your existence was no longer justified: the harsh rule was understood and acknowledged without dispute. The old chose their end by stepping off the back of the sledge while on a journey across the pack ice, or were abandoned on a hunting trip. Their death was accepted as inevitable by their children. They were not an emotive people but reserved and watchful. Their lives were hard. Obtaining enough food was an unremitting problem, worse in winter when game was scarcer to find. Sombre and withdrawn by nature, they could release emotion only by crying. Tears were a refuge to them, they could weep copiously whenever they wished – to do so purged and soothed them.

The *Quest* dropped off the families at their settlements as they passed. 'The stone winter houses were in a filthy state, with half-chewed bones and other refuse left lying since the previous winter,' says Chapman. 'The oldest Eskimo woman showed me with great pride a store of meat she possessed, cached in a stone enclosure: there were several seals with the blubber still attached, to which adhered hundreds of large bluebottle corpses.'

They surveyed the coast north of Angmagssalik for more than two hundred miles. The pack ice, which was constantly shifting in the wind and current, hindered the work of the flyers as well as the land parties who went off in a small boat for days at a time to map the various fjords. The work was done by Stephenson assisted by Courtauld and Chapman ('a charming chap but horribly hearty,' in Courtauld's view). It was Courtauld who captained the whale-boat – a job he was well suited for as he had been given his own 24-foot racing yacht while still at Cambridge. A shy man, he found social encounters agonising but was absolutely sure of himself in command of a boat.

The coast was clogged with brash and pack ice among which floated bergs, some the size of a city block. All were in continuous movement and all were eight times as big below the surface. Courtauld would steer standing up in the stern, looking out for the translucent sheen of submerged reefs. When he spotted one, he would throw the outboard into reverse while the others fended off with oars. They carried block and tackle to haul the boat up onto the ice should it become trapped. Pinched between two converging floes it would have been mercilessly crushed.

From hard-won positions on the precipitous shore they surveyed with plane table and range finder. At night they camped, finding a ledge in the bare rock that rose a steep two or three thousand feet from the sea. They cooked supper – ptarmigan, seal steak or salmon – and ate by the light of a moon that shone on a bloodless, frozen seascape. In the short night the only sound was the continuous grating mutter of the shifting ice.

Every day, Chapman hunted game for fresh meat to take back to the *Quest*. Opportunity presented itself unexpectedly. 'I was looking out for birds when I saw a long way ahead a yellowish-white object swimming in the water... I soon realised it was the head of a polar bear. The bear, looking very yellow beside the white ice, was swimming near a large iceberg... As we got nearer it dived, and at the same time the motor, which Courtauld was trying to run slowly, suddenly stopped. We were left with no power of steering the boat, making straight for the place where the bear would reappear. I was ready with the Mannlicher, when with a fierce roar the bear came up right under the bows. I saw its wicked little piggy eyes and its black snout a mere yard away. Luckily the first shot told and the great cream-coloured carcass sprawled in the water. When we reached the shore the corpse was so heavy that the three of us were quite unable to pull it out onto the sloping rocks, and I had an unpleasant two hours skinning the bear standing knee-deep in the icy water... An hour later another bear was seen. As we had been unable to secure any photographs of the first, we pursued it without any intention of shooting it... Stephenson and I were in the bows of the boat, gazing into the finders of our cameras, when all at once the motor stopped again. Suddenly I looked up and saw that in an amazingly short space of time the bear with great agility had clambered out onto an ice-floe and had turned snarling ready to attack. I dropped my camera and seizing the rifle which was ready loaded on the bows, took a snap shot at the bear just as he was about to leap into the boat. We were so near that as he fell forward stone-dead he almost upset the boat with the splash of his huge body.'

For Chapman, for all of them, the work they were doing and its motive, to open up an air route over unknown country, was inspiring. They were bonded in the same mission, and the elemental struggle to feed themselves and stay alive absorbed all their spare energy and imagination. 'Instincts inherent in man but dormant through long years of "civilisation" were called into play,' he says.

The day following the bear hunt was Courtauld's twenty-sixth birthday. That evening they put up the tent on a small ledge covered with crowberries, perched above the sea on the steep rocky flank of the mountain. Firing up the Primus, they cooked up a feast to celebrate the occasion as the sun sank behind the massif, spreading purple shadow across the ice-pack beneath them. They dined in the glow of a waning crescent moon that cast a ghostly greenish sheen over the pack, which stretched to the limit of their sight beyond the curve of the world.

MENU
Bear's Tongue Soup
Fried Fillet of Kangerdlugsuatsiak Trout
Seal's Kidney and Onions
Theodolite Sauce
Stewed Crowberries

Birthdays had special significance for Courtauld. He was close to neither of his parents; at home and at school he had been punished and beaten often. For the son of a rich man, his childhood was severe and he was anything but spoilt. But birthdays were commemorated as red-letter days, and on one of them he had been given his own 24-foot racing yacht. This evening, also, disclosed a wonder. While the three men were at dinner the dusk began to alter; the violet sky behind the mountains grew streaked with emerald shadows. Tentacles of flame flickered above the black line of the mountain crests. Loops and whorls of luminous colour shimmered and writhed over the heavens, climaxing in unearthly brilliance when a procession of mock suns swam across the sky, extinguishing the stars. None of Courtauld's birthdays came close to this one, when the gods staged for him the spectacle of the Northern Lights.

For a month the *Quest* sailed north, anchoring wherever they found open water. Then the seaplane was lowered over the side and Gino and D'Aeth went up to take survey photographs from 10,000 feet to supplement the work of the land party. Shooting overlapping pictures of that precipitous coastline of glaciers and mountains kept Gino busy, but he admitted to Scott he felt nervous. Every car he had owned had broken down continually and he had no confidence in anything mechanical. A failure in the Gypsy Moth's motor must mean disaster, and the open water they had used for take-off was not certain to still be there when they returned to land.

The Arctic summer was nearing its end. Each night the sea froze over and the Captain of the *Quest* was becoming restive. He didn't want to be trapped there for the winter. Nor did Gino; he had other plans. Nevertheless, when the photography was completed they pressed on northward through the ice to enter Kangerdlusuak, the Big Bay of the Eskimos. For thirty-five miles the fjord wound between stark mountains which framed the great glaciers at the head. Here the men made a cache of food, for Gino hoped to send a sledging party northward in the spring to survey the inside limit of the coastal mountains. Everyone was pleased as Punch, but most of all the Captain, for though many ships had tried to penetrate this fjord none had succeeded. Gino and Chapman climbed a hill from whose summit they could see the whole length of the fjord. 'It was an exhilarating thought that we were the first white men ever to behold that view,' Chapman said; and there was an even better 'first' to come.

In the cold oblique light of dawn, the ship's deck is rimmed with frost and the rigging glitters with a trim of icicles. The brief Arctic summer is coming to an end. It is now September and the new-formed ice covering the fjord each morning is thicker and takes longer to melt. The days are growing shorter; if the *Quest* is to get back to base before the pack traps them it is time to be gone. But before they sail Gino wants to complete one last flight north, this time not following the coastline but to photograph the landward edge of the coastal range.

He and D'Aeth are rowed out to the seaplane. D'Aeth takes the controls as Gino straps the mapboard to his thigh and secures the survey camera and a stack of photographic plates. Someone in the boat swings the propeller and the motor fires to life, coughing black smoke. The Gypsy Moth taxis across the water between the drifting floes – it's not easy to find a clear lead of sufficient length. When he does, D'Aeth heads the aircraft into the breeze and guns the motor to full power. The plane cuts across the surface feathering spray, skims, and lifts off. It climbs steeply to clear the coastal mountains and turns north. At an altitude of 10,000 feet they fly a path parallel to the shore but some sixty miles inland. The weather is clear, a pale blue sky tissued with wisps of cloud. Three thousand feet below them the jagged black peaks of the mountains run in a serrated line, holding in place the uniform white of the ice cap, which spreads away to the left of the aircraft as far as they can see; and further.

It is very cold in the open cockpits. The two men are wearing flannel shirts and sweaters beneath their flying jackets but the rush of air numbs their cheeks below the goggles. The roar of the engine is muffled by their helmets. They fly on while Gino exposes plates to compose an interlocking panorama of the mountains' profile. But the plane's fuel is dipping toward the halfway mark, soon they must turn back. Gino hunches down in the cockpit, goggles pushed up on his forehead to change plates. As he raises the camera to resume shooting a glitter on the other side of the aircraft catches his attention. He stares, blinks to clear his eyes, and looks again in disbelief. An apparition is taking shape high in the sky to the northeast. Far above the spread-out emptiness of the ice cap a majestic range of unknown mountains is rising into view. They tower far above the plane and for seconds he gazes at them in shock; then he bends forward to shout excitedly into the speaking tube connecting him to the pilot. D'Aeth banks the aircraft to head for the gleaming vision, which declares itself as they approach.

Coming nearer to the range, they see a frozen lake below, set high on a *massif* plateau backed by a line of peaks of immense height and grandeur. They rise far higher than the plane can climb. The tallest summit then known in Greenland is Petermann Peak at 10,000 feet, but these are much higher – between 15,000 and 17,000 feet, they calculate. D'Aeth banks the Moth to fly parallel to the mountain wall. Seams and wrinkles are etched by snow in the bald, granite face. Glaciers show like the glistening tracks of snails down the black rock. The crags tower above the tiny plane in gigantic spires. D'Aeth holds the aircraft straight and level while Gino exposes photograph after photograph, but the Moth is at its range, its fuel more than half gone. Reluctantly they bank and head for home.

* * *

Gino has discovered the highest mountains in the Arctic, later to be named the Watkins Mountains – not by him, he would name nothing after himself, but by the Danish Government. In the years that follow, several expeditions will try to reach and climb these mountains. None will succeed until a team (which includes two Everest men), put together and led by Courtauld in valedictory tribute, achieves the summit in 1935. But that will be an expedition undertaken in a more sombre and very different spirit to the mood of achievement, triumph and sheer exuberance shared by the young explorers aboard the *Quest* as, next morning, the little ship pulls anchor and steams south through the thickening pack ice on their 250-mile voyage back to base camp and the next phase of their adventure: the ice cap.

The Ice Cap

Five weeks earlier, in the middle of August, Scott and his party had halted on the slopes of the glacier leading up to the ice cap. Looking back they saw the *Quest* sail out of the bay and head north; then they turned their faces west and continued on their own journey to set up the weather station. Scott, the only man experienced in driving dog teams, was leader of the group. He had with him Rymill (who was responsible for navigation), Riley, Lindsay, and the doctor, Bingham. They took four sledges, each carrying a weight of 600 pounds and pulled by a team of seven dogs.

Early explorers were slow to learn that this was the only viable manner of travel in the Arctic. The sledge they did adopt but it took an age for them to appreciate the value of dogs to pull it. Every kind of motive power was tried before the practicality of the technique which the Eskimos had evolved over centuries overcame European and American prejudice against native methods. Peary, in his first attempt to reach the North Pole in 1909 by sledging over the pack ice, had his men put ropes over their shoulders to haul whale boats mounted on massive sledges. Nansen's party still man-hauled their sledges but wore skis to do so. Nordenskiold experimented with reindeer, but they had to be fed on moss which was bulky and required yet more reindeer to transport. Shackleton and Scott tried Manchurian ponies, but again their feed was bulky and the animals proved unable to endure such extreme weather conditions. As engine power for a sledge the husky is unbeatable. His food is compact; if hungry he will eat anything and, unlike the reindeer and horse, when dead he becomes food for the rest – and for his owner.

The forty-nine dogs Scott had bought in west Greenland had not been driven since he had acquired them. There had been no time to train them to work together in pairs on a single track, so the less efficient fan formation, with each dog on its own ten foot track, had to be employed. The snow covering the glacier had melted in the sun. The surface was bare ice – not smooth but ridged, prickly and sharp from rain. The wildly undisciplined dogs had to be dressed in canvas boots to protect their feet. The job of doing so and then harnessing them into sledge teams was exasperating beyond belief. The two-mile ascent up the steep waves of ice to the foot of Buggery Bank was slippery and uneven; both humans and dogs had difficulty remaining on their feet. Often it required all five men to advance one sledge. It took the whole day to reach the bottom of the bank. It began to rain. By the time they made camp among the huge blocks of ice at the base of Buggery they were short of breath, out of temper and soaking wet.

Next day they set to work hauling the equipment and supplies up the bank itself. The 300 yards of tumbled ice was so precipitous and slick that without wearing crampons it was impossible to stand up, let alone push a sledge. In their canvas boots the dogs could get little grip. With the men hauling on a rope and at the same time yelling at the dogs to pull, the half-loaded sledges were lugged toward the summit. Here Scott came into his own. Dressed in a rugger vest he had last worn for the Varsity Match of 1928, and which still bore his number on the back, he was everywhere, heaving, hauling, exhorting. Even before he had gained his Cambridge 'Blue' he had proved himself a team leader, captaining the First XV and First XI at Fettes. Throughout his childhood on the remote island of Mull, he had trained himself in toughness and endurance. He was in his element.

Two days were spent hauling eleven sledge-loads of material to the top of the bank. There they met with a labyrinth of crevasses. Scott and Rymill, roped together, went ahead, probing the slushy snow with poles to find a route through and marking it with flags. The next day the going was even slower. Both pathfinders put a foot through into enormous crevasses thinly bridged by snow. These crevasses became so numerous they had to go back to find another way around them. The following day this route too proved impossible and they had to retreat again. Visibility was poor, rain fell steadily. The temperature was high enough to melt the snow and they had to wade through thigh-deep rivers of icy water racing between the churned hummocks of ice.

On 17 August they still had not reached the head of the glacier; the way ahead was riddled with concealed crevasses. At one point the lead dog-team fell through the rotten surface, disappearing altogether in an instant. Their combined weight carried the sledge to the lip of the chasm before the driver could halt it. All seven dogs hung in the abyss, suspended in their traces. One by one they were hauled to the surface and the progress up the glacier resumed. During that day the temperature dropped to -3°C. Eventually they left the crevasses behind, the slope eased and by the time they made camp they had covered eight miles on firm snow. The way they had come was marked by coloured flags. They planted a large flag at the spot always known thereafter as Big Flag Depot. It was only fifteen miles from base but it had taken them six days to reach.

They were at an altitude of 6,000 feet. Behind them the summits of the coastal mountains had almost disappeared beneath the horizon; ahead stretched a slowly rising featureless plain of white – the ice cap.

Killing a dog which had become unmanageable, they buried it at Big Flag as emergency food for the future. Next day they reduced the dog teams' rations to three quarters and pressed on to establish the weather station. No rock, no tree, no bird broke the monotony of the view ahead. There existed no object for the eye to focus upon. They advanced into white nothingness, a void. Every half-mile they planted a flag to mark their route. Rymill went ahead on skis following a compass course into the void – steering almost due north in order to travel north-west because of the 45° magnetic variation this close to the Pole – and periodically stopping to take a back-bearing on their last flag. Next came Scott, who calculated the exact distance travelled from the last flag by means of a mileometer connected to a wheel behind his sledge. He was followed by a second compass-man taking bearings on the two ahead to keep them on a straight line of march. Behind him the last two sledge drivers planted the flags, set on bamboo poles driven into the snow.

Mostly the weather held good. Moving steadily uphill they covered twelve to fifteen miles each day. When mist or snow shut in they were unable to travel for they could not see the flags, so they made camp. Lindsay describes the routine:

Immediately the leader decides to halt for the night, the business of camping begins. First, the sledges are unlashed and the dogs are fed. Each one is given his lump of pemmican, which must be watched to its destination or, as soon as your back is turned, the tough dog of the team will steal from the others... Then two men put up the tent. As soon as it is up, the ground sheet, sleeping-bags, food-box and Primus stove are passed in through the doorway – a courtesy title for a hole that you can only just crawl through. The cook for the week at once arranges the inside of the tent and starts to get dinner ready. Meanwhile the other man fills the two saucepans with snow and passes them in. After this he takes a spade and piles up the snow all round the skirting of the tent, and puts more snow in front of the entrance within easy reach for replenishing the pots. His last job before turning in is to bring the skis, snowshoes and whips into the tent, so that the dogs cannot eat the raw hide on them during the night. By the time that he has had his last look round and is ready to go inside, the evening meal should be just about ready.

Buggery Bank had proved a ghastly start to their journey. Hauling the sledges up it had been an exhausting, nerve-wracking task; the dogs were exasperating and they themselves had become wet, uncomfortable and bad-tempered. But now they were on the ice cap and travelling and their mood changed. They felt well again and their spirits rose. At night Scott and Rymill occupied one tent, Riley, Lindsay and Bingham crowded into another. And so they dined. 'The greasy brown lumps of pemmican were put to float in the pot in company with the greasy yellow lumps of margarine; two spoonfuls of Plasmon and three of pea-flour were added, and then in ten minutes we had a hot meal... Pemmican is concentrated beef with added fat, margarine makes up half the ration. But after a hard day's sledging in cold weather, it always seemed to us that there could be nothing quite so good anywhere as those plates of hot stew.'

Each day they were climbing higher as they advanced further upon the ice cap; every night the aneroids registered another 500 feet above sea-level. Everyone was feeling the height; much more effort was needed to break camp in the morning and any sudden burst of energy left them breathless. The dogs, on three-quarter rations, were growing listless. On the eighteenth day of travel from the foot of the glacier they had reached the spot Gino had chosen for the weather station at a height of 8,600 feet and 112 miles in from Big Flag. Suspending an aerial between two skis upright in the snow, Rymill fiddled with the time-signal set. To his and everyone else's surprise it worked. Knowing the precise time by taking a sextant angle on the sun, they could establish their exact position.

They then erected the tent which would serve for living quarters at the weather station. Dome-shaped, of double canvas, it was nine feet in diameter and six high at the centre. Its entrance was a tunnel in the snow which, as it was below the level of the reindeer-carpeted floor, did not drain away heat from the interior.

Next they constructed three small igloos (two as storehouses, the other a latrine), which connected to the main tunnel through underground passages. Finally they set up the weather instruments: a cup anemometer for measuring the force of the wind, a nephescope to calculate the speed of clouds, maximum and minimum thermometers, two calibrated poles to gauge the fall of snow, and inside the tent a barograph and thermograph. This was state-of-the-art apparatus acquired by Gino from the Air Ministry, but one piece of equipment was conspicuously absent: a radio, or two-way wireless set as it was then called. The expedition possessed one but it weighed 600 pounds. Finding that it overloaded the sledges, at the last moment they had decided not to bring it.

Lindsay and Riley, who were to remain at the station, expected to be relieved in a month. They had a Primus stove, an Aladdin lamp, twenty-four gallons of paraffin and candles. Their food supply provided full rations for five weeks, but if necessary this could be made to last longer. That night all five explorers shared a celebratory dinner in the tent; they had fulfilled their purpose. Next morning, on the 30 August, Scott, Rymill and Bingham left to return to base, driving their sledges towards the rising sun. The weather was brilliant, the sun shone in a turquoise sky streaked with pink cloud. The way was signed by flags and all of it was downhill. The dogs were keen; they knew they were going home and, trained to work as a team now, they responded to the orders of the driver. The surface was firm powder snow. With Scott in the lead the three men rode on their sledges, brandishing their whips and cracking the twelve-foot lash above the dogs' heads to urge them faster, laughing and calling to each other above the hiss of the runners on the snow and stinging rush of ice crystals on their cheeks. The ice cap ahead was a sloping field of gold blazing in the sun. They covered forty-three miles before dark and were back at base in four days. Gino was already there, having flown ahead of the *Quest* in the seaplane; the rest of the survey group reached home on 16 September. All of them found the place had changed since they had left it almost a month before at the start of their various journeys.

Lemon, the radio operator and technician, had been left alone there at their departure. He was not alone when they returned. On the day the *Quest* sailed north for Kangerlugsuak three girls and an Eskimo boy had turned up at the base. All were got up in their best clothes, the girls wearing ornamental seal-fur trousers, close-fitting blouses and short beaded capes. Giggling and shy, they offered to help. The base hut and the area around it were a chaotic mess and Lemon put them to cleaning the place up. The boy humped wood and coal; the girls scrubbed out the hut, sewed curtains and cooked. They wanted to stay. Lemon liked the idea but was unsure how some of the other men would react; he didn't want to compromise himself. That evening reluctantly he put them all in a motorboat to run them home to the settlement a few miles away. Almost at once the outboard motor broke down. Taking this as a sign from on high, he rowed back to base and installed them in the loft.

When Scott's party and the *Quest's* surveyors got back, they 'found the base like a well-organised country house, with central heating, electric light and almost all modern conveniences,' says Chapman. 'Everything was beautifully clean and in its right place, and the Eskimo staff equally immaculate... The natives did all the cleaning, laid the table, washed up and did a vast amount of sewing. When we sat down to meals they brought the dishes round to the left side as if they had been used to it all their lives. Lemon gave all his orders in Eskimo, and they were promptly obeyed – it all looked too easy.'

But it had not been so. Lemon had had a trying time while the others were away. The base was equipped with a range of weather instruments similar to those at the ice cap station, but to read and record these every three hours had been among the easier of his tasks. His radio schedule involved morse contact with the *Quest* three times a day and – in theory – periodic contact with the Government Wireless Station in Aldershot, which was their official link with Britain. For whatever reason this link did not work; no signal penetrated the ether either way, and the Air-Route Expedition's only sporadic contact with their homeland was by way of an amateur ham radio freak perched on a hill in northern England who relayed their messages when he happened to be there to receive them.

The transmitter frequently broke down; repairing it occupied several of Lemon's mornings. In between these various duties he was fitting up the photographic darkroom, installing a sink, and wiring the hut for electric light to run off the generator. A capable and practical man used to army discipline and imposing order, all these things were more or less within his control. The dogs were not. The dogs were a nightmare. Twenty-one of them were away with Scott on the ice cap, the rest marooned on an island in the bay. There they were fed once a day, but it had struck no one they would swim ashore as a pack to roam wild and scavenge. They ate everything including wire mesh. They consumed sealskin boots, clothes and floor covering; they plundered the fish store and looted the whale-meat pen. Lemon's base log records with weary regularity: 'Dogs broke into whale-meat pen. Mended pen… mended pen… mended pen.' He gave up on trying to corral them and let the beasts run loose.

Lack of radio contact with England did not trouble the young explorers for none of them – except Courtauld, occasionally – was missing home. The base hut was a crowded but delightful common room to live in. Lindsay thought they got on so well 'because most of them were gentlemen and only three hadn't been to public schools.' The group shared the same background and purpose, but not all shared the same views – or tastes. No one voiced their annoyance for a long while, but the live-in presence of the Eskimo women posed a bit of a problem from the beginning. Arpika was the oldest, most sensible and the best shot. 'If you take her out after ptarmigan you do well to give her your gun,' Lindsay noted. Tina, the youngest, was 'an incredibly sluttish and dirty girl' who had the habit of cleaning the plates and pans by spitting on them and wiping them with her fingers. Gertrude, her older sister, was the prettiest and most temperamental. 'A sex-conscious young woman, highly strung and inclined to be tiresome,' says Chapman – who next year would father a son by her.

Eskimos seemed to the explorers to have an open attitude to sex – hardly surprising as there were no newspapers, radio or TV, no alcohol, no Public School system, no diversion of any kind, and a large part of the year was passed in continuous, freezing night. Over the countless long winters compounding Eskimo history, games and pastimes had developed that were suitable to the dark. There was some inequality between the sexes. Chastity was periodically imposed upon women, while men were always free to be promiscuous. Wife-swapping was a common practice. Far from causing friction between the males, the Danish ethnologist Birket-Smith believes, 'The husbands feel that... it is one of the most effective ways they can enhance and strengthen a friendship.' The sex parties held to celebrate the end of a period of mourning or a successful hunt involved only couples. Single men and the few surviving oldsters were excluded, literally left out in the cold. The explorer Harold Moltke stresses the festive nature of these parties. 'The group exchange... took place after a five-day mourning period. A meal was organised, to be attended by everyone; the food was provided by a hunter who had left the village before the mourning taboo period began. To celebrate the feast and the liberation of the village to the full, it was decided to exchange wives... The happy children were beside themselves. They ran from one tent to another, very preoccupied by their parents' arrangements.'

Eskimo men seemed not to suffer from jealousy; they were not proprietorial. When whaling and sealing ships first came to the Arctic their crews found the women approachable, their men relaxed, even welcoming the transaction, and glad of the small benefits which resulted. Lemon was the first to take an Eskimo lover. Gino followed, then Chapman. Scott and Courtauld were not comfortable with the arrangements. Sleeping with the natives was not the way Englishmen behaved; they thought it was demeaning. But Lindsay was particularly affronted:

He believed what a man got up to in London or Paris was all very well, but in a crowded hut on an Arctic expedition he didn't fancy it for himself and objected to it in others. All winter he had an Eskimo woman climbing over him to reach Watkins in the bunk above and by next summer he had had enough. In Greenland there was always the danger of the relief ship not getting through the pack ice. If that happened, and they faced a second winter in the hut, he meant to protest to Watkins about his public love life, and tell him to pitch a tent elsewhere and take his women with him.'

But at this stage nobody objected out loud about the matter. These were early days for the expedition. Some of its members had been tried a little physically, but none had been put to the test emotionally. Though the nights were drawing in around the dormitory they shared in such close proximity, winter had not yet shut them in, nor could they imagine what monsters might roam in the frozen dark which was to come.

Well, I'd Eat *You*

In early autumn, the *Quest* sailed from Iceland – not for any purpose of discovery, but to pick up the Expedition's luggage inadvertently left behind on their departure for the Arctic. This was not due to Gino's incompetence, but de Havilland's. While unloading the second Gypsy Moth from the *Gustav Holm* it was found that the ski undercarriages for both aircraft had been forgotten in England. The problem of lost baggage is always troublesome, but arrangements to regain these were complicated by the fact that morse messages in both directions between base camp and Farnham had to be relayed via the ham operator only intermittently available on his hilltop in northern England.

On the same day as the *Quest* sailed for Iceland, Gino and Scott started with two dog teams for the ice cap station. They were followed by a second group consisting of Bingham and D'Aeth (who would relieve the couple manning it), with two others. A support party helped them winch their heavily loaded sledges up Buggery Bank, accompanying them far as Big Flag before returning to base.

The hut became an infinitely more spacious and comfortable

place with only three men living there – plus of course the Eskimo staff in the loft who now outnumbered them. A few days later Chapman and Lemon took the three girls to visit the small settlement six miles down the coast where they lived. They started off in high spirits but, as always, the boat's outboard motor broke down within minutes. To reach their destination they rowed the overcrowded craft through a surreal graveyard of decaying icebergs eroded into fantastic sculptures, their grotesque forms rotting in the last warmth of the year.

The four or five families forming the settlement had only just returned from a summer passed in tents, hunting and fishing further along the coast. When Chapman, Lemon and the girls turned up they were busy putting up the winter house which they would all share for the next seven months. The permanent part of this, four walls built of boulders and paved with flat stones, was commonly owned. The method of living the Eskimos had evolved over centuries – the only practicable method of survival in these hostile conditions – was communism. The land, the sea, the hunting areas and the larger boats belonged to the group. Only the hunting gear, kayaks, sledges, weapons and dogs were individually owned. The wooden sections of the common house, the window frames, roof beams and sleeping bench, were being fitted into place under the direction of Arpika's father when Chapman, Lemon and the girls arrived at the settlement.

Gertrude and Tina took the two explorers to visit their mother, Potardina, in the tent she shared with her four other daughters and an orphan boy she had adopted. 'The occupants had already gone to sleep,' says Chapman, 'but were delighted to see us and produced some cold cod and sugar from under the sleeping-bench.'

Although the external temperature was below zero, it was warm enough inside. The tents were made of sealskins hung over a frame of driftwood poles. In those of the 'richer' families (where the males were the best hunters) a see-through curtain was strung across the doorway, made from strips of translucent seal intestines. At the rear of the tent a wooden sleeping platform was raised on stones a foot above the ground and thickly covered with seal furs. Above the platform hung a wooden rack for drying clothes. Pots and pans suspended from the poles could be slid along to dangle directly over the cooking stove. Lighting was provided by soapstone blubber lamps.

The two men sat down on some boxes, Lemon produced his makeshift vocabulary and conversation began. 'They seemed very jovial people, always ready to burst out laughing, and after the first few minutes showed no sign of shyness,' Chapman said. Leaving Potardina's, they called on the other tents and woke the families inside. Small, dark, prematurely wrinkled faces emerged from piles of skin and fur; their owners smiled with inscrutable blank eyes and made them welcome. In one tent they were given a snack of cold seal meat, in another a tin of blackberries was passed around. Conversation was limited, 'but the women were amazed at our clothes and simply enraptured by our zip fasteners.' At the end of the evening the explorers invited the younger women back to their place. Arpika, Gertrude, Tina, six others, and the two men squeezed into a tent designed for two. The fit was snug. 'Abandoning all conversation,' as Chapman puts it, this heap of warm bodies, piled up and interlaced, passed the time dunking ship's biscuits into extra sweet cocoa... then went to sleep. Or so he claims.

Meanwhile, up on the ice cap, the weather stayed fine. Gino, Scott, and their companions reached the ice cap station to find the two occupying it in good health and spirits but extraordinarily pleased to see them. All eight of them packed into the ice-station's tent to share a celebration meal, sing alpine mountain songs, and fall asleep in a warm fug of tobacco smoke. Next day Bingham and D'Aeth set up home in the weather station. Gino told Rymill to lead the others back to base and then send Chapman up to the ice cap with a large sledge party, wireless equipment and as much food as they could haul to provision the station for winter. Then Gino and Scott set off on an expedition to the south.

They were pressed for time. Each day was shorter than the last; soon the good weather must break and it would become hard, even impossible, to travel on the ice cap in the darkness and storms of winter. Before the weather deteriorated, Gino wanted to complete a long sledge journey south down the middle line of the ice cap to discover if a traverse valley ran across the country, which might allow an aircraft to cross it at a lower altitude. Having established whether or not this existed, he planned to return to base along the line of the coastal mountains, plotting their height as they travelled.

He and Scott started on their journey with two sledges, fourteen dogs, and food for six weeks. The weather was fair, but the surface of the featureless frozen plain they moved across was ridged and difficult. For the first three days they travelled at just over one mile an hour. But men and dogs were eating 20 pounds weight each day; the sledges would grow lighter as they progressed and they still hoped to survey 200 miles south before having to turn back. The going was bad, but also the dogs were pulling less well than before. Weakened from half-rations on the journey to the station, they showed little spirit. Instinctively, perhaps, they sensed the imminent threat of winter better than the men did. At dawn on the fourth day, Gino and Scott crawled out of the tent into an opaque void of drifting snow. Harnessing the reluctant dogs, they travelled on by compass into the nothingness. The wind had whipped the surface into corrugated waves which overturned the sledges continually. The next day was unseasonably warm, but in the night the temperature dropped.

The sudden change made the dogs listless and apathetic. To revive them, Gino decided to give them extra food – which could only come from their own rations. 'And it's a particularly good idea,' he said to Scott, 'For the dogs won't want the chocolate and sugar. We'll have a grand feast tonight.' That evening Scott was cook. The paraffin stove was fuming as it sometimes did at altitude, but the tent was tightly closed. 'We never had any nonsense about fresh air under those conditions,' Scott says. Gino, whose eyes watered easily, was lying face down by the tent wall while Scott knelt above the stove sprinkling porridge oats into the pan of pemmican to make it even more delicious when… the next thing he knew he was lying on his back in the snow outside looking at the stars and his head hurt like hell. Sick and cold, he crawled back into the tent to find Gino squeezing pemmican stew from his sodden sleeping bag. 'What happened?' he asked.

The stove had used up the oxygen in the tent, forming carbon monoxide, and Scott kneeling above it had been knocked out cold. Gino, lying on the ground, had not been affected, but if he had stood upright when he was dragging Scott outside, he would also probably have passed out for the gas is odourless and quickly fatal. His calmness and quick thinking had saved the other's life but as Scott says, 'You cannot thank a man when he starts cursing you for ruining a good dinner.'

For the next two weeks they sledged south down the spine of the ice cap but their pace was infuriatingly slow. The dogs were lethargic, coming to a stop and sitting down every fifty yards. Even after extra food and a day's rest they performed no better. It was puzzling, for the cause was not clear. Both Gino and Scott had experience of driving dog teams, though not on the ice cap, but their knowledge did not come close to that rapport which the Eskimo people enjoyed with their dogs. Driver and team depended on each other; if either got it wrong, all died.

Gino's and Scott's dogs grew so apathetic it was almost impossible to get them to pull, they seemed exhausted. Rations for both men and beasts were almost half gone and what had been tiresome was becoming alarming. If they were to get back to base they must turn for home at once, Gino decided. Next day they headed back north-west for the coastal mountains. Instantly the dogs revived, their tails came up and they broke into a trot. On skis the men couldn't keep up with them, so they rode on the sledges. It was like that for the next two days. The men were disappointed: they had got nowhere, accomplished nothing and would reach home with uneaten rations. It was inexplicable and odd; they puzzled about the reason that evening over supper in the tent.

At midnight they were asleep when something struck the canvas so hard it sounded like a bomb exploding. They jerked awake, bolt upright in their sleeping bags. A pause. Then the tent began to flap and shake as if it were being beaten with sticks by a shrieking mob outside. A wind stronger than anything they had ever known, ever believed possible, hurled down upon them. The assault went on and on, the gale blew without let-up for the next fifty hours. The dogs rolled themselves up, faces covered by their tails, and soon were buried beneath the snow. When the men parted the tent's entrance to peer out the view was a torrent of white, a mass of snow rushing past in a driven spume so dense they could hardly breathe in it.

Inside the sealed tent it was noisy but quite cosy. Warm in their sleeping bags they could eat and doze and read. Gino had already finished the two books he had brought with him, Trevelyan's *History of England* and an anthology of short stories, so he borrowed Scott's *Oxford Book of English Verse* and re-read his favourites. They talked. Gino spoke of the journey they would make next summer, when travel again became possible, from the base to Ivigtut on the south coast, a distance of 500 miles. He talked too, says Scott, 'of buying dogs in Labrador and travelling westward along the Arctic coasts of Canada and Siberia till we rounded the North Cape (Gino always included his listener in these schemes) and turned south into Europe, with the skin peeling off our faces from sunburn and frostbite, to enjoy the luxury of some big town. That would be training for a similar journey round the coasts of Antarctica. Then there was Mount Everest which he said had never been climbed chiefly because it had been considered as a mountaineering rather than a bad weather problem...'

On the third morning the wind dropped. They dug out the dogs and travelled on into the drifting void, but the animals were weak from discomfort and sleeplessness. That afternoon the gale returned, pinning them down for a further thirty-six hours. When it eased they started again at once for good travelling conditions were becoming rare. The wind blasted down the slope of the ice cap across their path. The dogs were always trying to veer away from it, and in gusts a sledge lifted out of the hands of a man struggling to control it. To put up the tent that evening in the full force of the gale was a nightmare. By the time they succeeded in piling the sledge and all their ration boxes on the skirting to stop it from blowing away they were exhausted.

Next morning visibility was again poor but they pressed on. A dull mist infused the day, the light was fogged and shadowless. The weather was warm and the wind crust forming the surface was not quite firm enough to bear the weight of a man without snowshoes. Late in the afternoon one of Scott's bindings came undone and he let go of the sledge while the dogs went on. He was a few yards behind when they topped a crest to come upon a downhill slope; they started to trot. 'I yelled "Unipok, stop!"' says Scott, 'But they either would not hear or did not understand – it was a command which had been unnecessary for many weeks. I could not move fast enough in snowshoes so I took them off, but only to find that the crust would not bear my weight. By now the sledge was far ahead and on it was the tent, my sleeping-bag and a large proportion of the food. I turned and shouted to Gino, thinking that he might be able to catch my dogs by whipping up his own. But they would not respond.'

Gino took off his snowshoes and started to run. He ran lightly, with quick short steps; but even so he broke through the crust every four or five yards. At first he gained rapidly; but as he began to grow tired the distance between him and Scott's sledge remained much the same. Several times he made a sprint but just before he reached the handlebars he stumbled through the crust on which the dogs ran easily. It began to grow dark. Gino knew that he must catch up soon or not at all. Without a tent and with only one sleeping-bag between them they would perish in another storm. He made a final effort, dived for the sledge, caught it and held on. The dogs, as if tired of the game, stopped and lay down at once.

'Damn you Scott,' said Gino when the other caught up with him, 'I'd taken a lot of trouble to stay cool all day and now I'll have to sit up half the night to dry my clothes.' He was dripping with sweat though the temperature was below zero. Scott said he was sorry, but at least they had done an extra mile or two in the right direction. Gino laughed and did not refer to it again, but afterwards he admitted that this had been one of the most anxious occasions of his life.

Gino had plenty of time to dry his clothes. In the next six days they travelled only fourteen miles, and that advance was made almost entirely during one calm spell. For the rest of the time they lay in their sleeping-bags while the wind thrashed the tent unmercifully and hid everything outside in drift. Worried about their food situation, they slept very little. It was like trying to sleep during an artillery bombardment. The violence and noise of it were obliterating. The wind slammed into the tent, grabbed it in its teeth, and shook it as a dog shakes a rat to kill it. Curled in their sleeping-bags they lay there, battered by the assault. To the two men the forces against them seemed incalculable. They were on a vast ice plateau thousands of feet thick with a wind blasting across it, bounding down in great gusts toward the sea. The wind was huge, they were flecks in its path. Insignificant, irrelevant details to be blown away.

'This is a damned silly way to spend one's time,' Gino said, 'and these storms are pretty certain to get worse. We ought to be lying in our bunks with an Eskimo playing the gramophone and feeding us with seal meat and milk chocolate.' Scott rose to this, as Gino knew he would. What the hell had Gino expected, starting on a long sledge journey this late in the year? he demanded. When he had thought in England about the expedition, had he really expected it to be a bed of roses? And why was he now being so negative and frightening by speaking of still more terrible weather ahead instead of looking for the bright side of things?

'I had to make things sound attractive or no one would have come,' said Gino. 'But now we are here it's just as well to be ready for anything.' He sat up and rubbed his back. 'I'm getting bed sores, let's see if we can travel.'

It was dusk outside the tent but a diffused greenish glow of moonlight filtered through the driving snow to cast moving shadows across the ice field. It took four hours to dig out the boxes, load the sledges and harness the dogs which were sometimes hard to find, for the drift blinded the men and made everything twice as heavy. Then they started across the storm. The dogs pulled well, they were as keen as the men to reach home, but the surface was soft and the going slow. In the dim light the lead dog was no more than a ghostly shadow trotting into the void. The wind blasted across their path; clutching the handlebars of the sledges they had to bend double against its force. The tempest lashed the ground, snatching

up the loose snow into separate streams that snaked in one direction
then another, sometimes crossing over each other as if they were
two different roads. The ground they stumbled over in their clumsy
snowshoes was insubstantial, undulating; nothing stayed firm or
fixed. In the different streams of snow writhing past them they
could *see* the wind, and they saw it was not one thing but legion.

When Gino had questioned the Eskimos about the ice cap, via the
mixed-race interpreter, they had shown dismay at his plans to travel
on it. They spoke of malign spirits who inhabited the desolation
and devils living within the wind. He and the other Europeans had
dismissed these tales as fanciful superstition and native folklore.
But now he and Scott met these demons. They *saw* them. The wind
was not a constant force. It blew fiercely then rested briefly as if
gathering strength. For a few moments of false calm it emitted a
sullen whine which turned into a chesty rattle, a loud hoarse intake
of breath. Then it roared out in all its force. Small whirlwinds
spiralled into existence, sucking up the snow into the moving forms
of giants who spun toward them, cuffing and buffeting them as they
rampaged past. Each time the gusts hurtled towards them the same
thing happened. The dogs turned away downwind and the sledge
skidded round to meet them. It was as if a stick had been broken in
the middle. They straightened out the line, then the sledges blew
over and the dogs lay down. They tried again but it was hopeless.
Gino waited for Scott to draw up and halt beside him. Both teams
of dogs lay down in their traces, curled up with their backs to the
wind and went to sleep. 'We can't travel in this,' Gino said. 'We'd
better make camp.'

Crouched against the storm, they unharnessed the dogs with
frozen fingers and unloaded the sledges. It took them hours to pitch
the tent. Inside they lay down without taking off their clothes. For a
little while they discussed their position which had become serious.
They had very little food left and the dogs were being weakened by

every storm; they must travel again within twenty-four hours. If it were still blowing they could only go down-wind. That would take them to the mouth of the big ice valley where there were certain to be crevasses, hidden by drift. Beyond them they would find a mountainous, deeply indented coastline along which they would have to walk northwards carrying their loads, for the sea would be still unfrozen. On the other hand, they were only about thirty miles in a straight line from the Big Flag Depot and the marked route to the base; a calm spell would see them there. Therefore, if the storm weakened, they would race for home; if not, they would run with the wind and trust to luck. Meanwhile the tempest was getting worse. When their rations ran out they could start to kill the dogs to feed the others and themselves, but it would require a dog per day to do so. With the dogs gone they would be unable to make it back to base.

Starvation is a recurring theme in the history of Arctic exploration; cannibalism an occupational hazard. In extremity it becomes necessary to eat your companion(s). In 1881, fifty years before Gino's expedition, Lieutenant Greely, an officer in the US Fifth Cavalry Regiment, was put in charge of twenty-four men at the American Polar Station on Ellesmere Island, then the most northerly base in the Arctic. Although set up by the American government, it was poorly equipped, yet Greely proved very effective. The magnetic, meteorological, oceanographic, zoological and botanical observations he recorded were the most comprehensive to date. By the end of summer 1882 the party had completed their mission and were preparing to return home, but the ship sent to get them was halted by ice in Smith Sound and could not reach them. Nothing could be done to relieve them during that winter but in the spring of 1883 the US government despatched a second ship, *The Proteus*. It was wrecked on the coast 200 miles south of their position.

Greely was a capable officer, but a strict disciplinarian who had been disliked by his men even before their present difficulties set in. He and his second-in-command, Lieutenant Kilingsbury, were no longer on speaking terms and communicated only by written notes. By now the party had been expecting a relief ship for two years and were desperately low on food, subsisting on the occasional kill made by the two Eskimo hunters attached to the group. There were angry disagreements over what they were to do until Greely imposed his authority; on his orders they crowded into two canoes and their only dinghy and headed south down the uninhabited east coast of Ellesmere Island. The sea was obstructed by ice; their passage slow, but at the start of October they came upon the wreckage of the *Proteus* and a cache of food containing bread, canned meat and some tea, together with a message from the ship's captain saying that the US government had not given up on them and would send another ship; they must keep up their courage and await rescue. Greely accordingly set up camp at this spot for their third winter in the Arctic. The 'hut' they occupied was the upturned whole boat; they had provisions for forty days.

They were doomed to remain here for the next eight months. At first the Eskimos caught a few foxes which they shared, and they foraged for small shrimps along the shoreline, but when the ice froze solid this was no longer possible and they fed on lichens scraped from the rocks. Their clothes were ripped to tatters, their physical condition infirm, some were suffering from scurvy and all from frostbite. They quarrelled continuously and the minds of some started to slip and become confused. One after another they began to expire, in all eighteen would die.

Greeley's diary records:

May 20: in order to give Israel [the astronomer] the last chance, and on Dr Pavy's recommendation, four ounces of the raven was given him today, that being our only meat...

May 23: Ralston died about 1 a.m. Israel left the [shared] sleeping bag before his death, but I remained until about 5 a.m., chilled through by contact with the dead...

May 26: How we live I do not know, unless it is because we are determined to. We all passed an exceedingly wretched night... We were yet fourteen in number, but it was evident that all soon must pass away...

June 4: We had not strength enough to bury Salor, so he was put out of sight in the ice-foot... Our condition grows more horrible every day...

June 6: Henry admitted that he had taken... seal-skin thongs; and further, that he had a bundle, concealed somewhere, of seal-skin. He... showed neither fear nor contrition. I ordered him shot, giving the order in writing... Everyone, without exception, acknowledged that Henry's fate was merited...

June 8: Obliged to eat the last seal-skin thongs in stew this afternoon, with which we mixed the Tripe de Roche [lichen] and reindeer moss... seal-skin gloves for dinner. Elison expressed a desire that his arms and legs should go to the Army Medical Museum in the interests of science. His case is most singular.

Elison's frostbitten limbs were gangrenous and there was little chance his wishes would be respected. For many weeks the survivors had been eating the corpses of the dead. The party of ragged bearded men huddled beneath the upturned boat had regressed to sub-humans; squatted in their chill and filthy den, the eyes in their wasted faces glared ravenously at the man most likely next to die. Pavy, the expedition's doctor, butchered the dead bodies with a scalpel, stripping the flesh from the bone. Thighs, arms and legs were cut up for the cooking pot; hands, feet and faces were left intact. He performed this work on many corpses before the task so unhinged him he committed suicide by swallowing what remained of their medical supplies, then threw himself into the sea so he would not be eaten himself. After he had gone the last restraints of civilisation were discarded. Skeletons were picked clean of flesh, the men gnawed their comrades' bones, cracking them between stones to extract the marrow before flinging the refuse on the beach. The scattered remains could not be reassembled.

On 22 June, Greely noted:

> Near midnight... I heard the sound of the whistle noise of the *Thetis*... I feebly asked Brainard and Long if they had the strength to get out... but nothing was to be seen... Suddenly strange voices were heard calling me...

They belonged to men from an American rescue ship who came ashore to see two hairy forms they thought at first to be seals dragging themselves toward them over the rocks. Soon after, they came to a misshapen tent and could hear groans coming from within. One of the sailors was so overcome by dread at the sound he broke down in tears. Unable to find the entrance to the tent they slashed it open with a knife.

> What we saw before us was a horrifying spectacle. On one side, near the door, his head facing outside, a man was lying, apparently already dead. His jaw hung down and he looked at us with his eyes open, fixed and glassy, his lips lifeless. On the other side was another man, alive but with no hands or feet, with a spoon attached to the stump of his right arm... Opposite us, walking on his hands and knees, was a black man with a long tangled beard wearing a dirty, torn robe and a little red skull-cap, his eyes fixed and shining. When

Lieutenant Colwell appeared [adjutant on the *Thetis*] he got up and put on his glasses. 'Who are you?' Colwell asked him. The man did not answer and looked at him with a vacant expression. 'Who are you?' he asked again.

One of the men looked up. 'That's Greely, Major Greely.' Then Colwell crawled toward him and taking him by the hand said to him: 'Greely... Could it really be you?'

The storm had not let up and was still buffeting the tent where Gino and Scott lay in their sleeping bags, while their hungry dogs slept curled up and buried beneath the snow outside. The wind was blowing even more ferociously. They realised that its note had changed, the tone had altered to become a hoarse congested roar. There was something childishly terrifying about the noise, it sounded like the bellowing of an enraged giant. When they crawled from their bags to peer out from the flap the sight was the same, a spate of driven snow hurtling past in a solid mass. There seemed no reason the storm would ever stop. It was so hard to hear what the other said they relapsed into silence. An abnormally violent slam of wind would jerk them back into the present, but their minds were on home. Gino's thoughts were of his family and Nanny who, if he died on the ice cap, would be left to fend for themselves in England. His worries were imbued with guilt, particularly when they touched upon his sister. Without education and hardly any money, insecure and timid by nature, she was the least equipped to survive. He leaned across to say to Scott, 'If anything happens to me, look after Pam.'

Scott nodded in assent, suddenly very wide awake. Then Gino went on to say that if he were the first to die he would expect to be eaten. Scott was horrified by the remark though he didn't show it; to evince horror – or any other powerful emotion – was debarred by the code. As he describes it, he 'demurred'. 'Well I'd eat you,' Gino told him cheerfully, 'but then of course you're much more fat and appetising'.

Outside the tent the wind was blowing in gusts of a hundred miles an hour. The canvas smacked and bellied with each blow, the bamboo poles creaked and bent under the pressure. If anything gave way they would be flung into the chaos to struggle blindly and to die. But they had already done all they could to make the tent secure; the situation was beyond their control so they tried to forget it by re-reading their books. Yet their thoughts were always straying back to their position. Then Gino suggested they should read aloud to each other instead of to themselves. 'He began,' says Scott, 'With Dickens' *Christmas Carol* which was in a way seasonable; but that did not matter very much, for the peculiar virtue of reading aloud is unrelated to the story. It is the association of childhood, of a time when one was utterly helpless yet perfectly trustful and content...'

Scott had known such moments when his parents read to him, but not for long. They had ended when he was six and his father, an Edinburgh lawyer, was appointed a judge in the Egyptian High Court, and his parents sailed to live in Cairo, leaving him in an English boarding school. As the blizzard roared Gino read aloud; says Scott, 'his listener only failed to listen attentively because his thoughts were wandering in the past. We were utterly helpless, yet, for the present, perfectly trustful and content.'

At midnight the storm died. There was a fierce gust of wind – then quiet. A few vicious little kicks as of a dying animal, then complete silence. 'We had better get on,' said Gino. After a few minutes he decided to take only one sledge so that a man would be free to look after the vehicle while the other drove the dogs. They dumped all they could spare. It was striking how casually Gino could throw away things which were valuable but no longer strictly needed, Scott says. He was shocked to see his fine copy of the *History of England* lying in the snow with its pages flicking over in the wind.

With a double team on one sledge they travelled fast most of the night and camped while it was still dark. But when they went on again after an hour and a half of sleep they found themselves among a maze of thinly bridged crevasses. Gino went in front. He walked northward, dodging crevasses, taking them away from the great windy valley and back to the line of flags, stretching from the weather station to the base, that would guide them home. Next day the visibility was too bad to allow travel but there was practically no wind and the soft tapping of the snowflakes on the tent was pleasantly restful.

The following morning they woke to a huge silence – the wind was gone. They scrambled up, harnessed the dogs and got on the move. The day was misty and they travelled through a miasma of diffused light, the only sound the creak of leather and soft hiss of the sledge runners in the snow. Then in the shadowless void ahead, Gino glimpsed a fleck of colour, tiny yet momentous in significance. He halted his dogs to pick it up. It was a piece of scarlet thread, frayed from one of the expedition's flags. They realised they must be near the line of markers which would lead them home! Relief flooded through them, their troubles seemed over. Then far off in the shadowless all-white panorama they saw a broken black line which gradually resolved itself into men and sledges. They stared at the sight in astonishment; it had to be Chapman and his party returning from their journey to supply the ice cap station for the winter. To meet up with them in that vast spread of empty nothingness was an extraordinary coincidence. Thrilled by the encounter Gino and Scott hurried toward the first living creatures they had seen for six weeks. Their dogs quickened their pace, barking excitedly as they rushed toward the other party, which like themselves was moving. But – and both men realised it at the same instant – *travelling in the wrong direction.* Chapman's party was sledging west, not east, not returning home but still headed *for* the weather station and into the chaos of wind and night upon the ice cap from which they themselves had only just escaped.

WHO IN THIS WORLD IS

REALLY HAPPY?

GINO'S LAST INSTRUCTIONS to Chapman eight weeks earlier when he and Scott set out on their southern journey, were to assemble a large party of men and dogs to transport supplies and the wireless set to the ice cap station in order to provision it, and to install the two men who would staff it through the winter until they could be relieved the following spring. Chapman had begun to prepare for this mission as soon as he had got back to base. There the two pilots busy constructing a hangar for the airplanes hurried to complete their work before the gales of winter, while the rest portaged stores and equipment to the foot of the glacier in readiness for Chapman's journey.

By buying a scratch team of local dogs from the Eskimo settlement Chapman managed to assemble six teams, though he says some of them looked as if they had escaped from a circus. His relief party consisted of Courtauld, Lemon, Hampton, Stephenson and Wager. None except for himself had any experience in dog driving. On 26

October they were finally ready to start. After hours of maddening exasperation spent trying to catch the dogs, the rest of the day was passed ferrying men, animals and kit across the fjord in the motor boat. A support group of three accompanied them, who would assist them as far as the depot at Big Flag.

They found that the wind had blown almost all the snow off the glacier, leaving it smooth as glass. They pitched their tents on what snow remained and piled ration cases on the flaps to secure them. What followed is recounted in Chapman's diary:

27 October. Big wind in night. Alarm off 4 a.m. We collected the dogs. I saw my wild dog asleep with the rest of the team and, stalking him behind a rock, just got hold of his tail as he made off. He bit my thigh. Wind increased after lunch and reached gale force. The tent Lemon and I are sharing went down twice. 28 October. A terrible night. Turned in at 4.30 with the wind blowing furiously... We drove a metal spike to the ice to hold our tent and put 600 lb. of cases on the flap. The tent canvas strained and flapped... and to speak to each other across a gap of only a couple of feet we had to shout as loud as we could. Every few minutes tins of dog fat and other objects came tinkling down the ice past our tent and over the edge. Just below our tent the ice fell away, getting steeper and steeper till it finished in an ice-shoot over a frozen waterfall into the rocky gorge below the glacier. We dressed and put on our boots, knowing the tent could not stay much longer. At about 11 p.m. the end came. After a gust of prodigious force the outer cover blew away, scattering boxes over the edge as it went. We hung onto the poles of the inner tent for a few seconds, being lifted bodily off the ground. Fearing it would carry us down the glacier we let it go... I warned the others to stand to in boots and windproofs. I got into a tent with

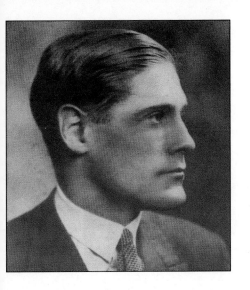

Clockwise from top left: Scott, Courtauld, Chapman and Gertrude, 'a young woman very conscious of her charms,' who bore Chapman a son.

Wintering with the Eskimos. *The explorers were warmly welcomed into an Eskimo winter house and assigned places on the communal sleeping bench. 'What struck me most tangibly on entering was the appalling smell of rotten sealmeat, urine, dogs and children, which was utterly nauseating when encountered for the first time.'*

Gino hunting. *The explorers had brought with them only basic supplies, intending to live like the Eskimos. Gino spent time hunting alone for meat to feed his tribe.*

On the ice. *They hunted in kayaks, but it was still possible to travel on foot by jumping from floe to floe. Their only dangerous rivals in the search for food were polar bears.*

Exploration by land, sea and sky. *They sailed north in the* Quest *to reconnoitre Greenland's coastal mountains, carrying a seaplane on deck to support the work of the land party. They discovered an unknown range, the highest peaks in the Artic.*

Scott and his dogs. *Gino planned to set up a weather station in the country's unexplored interior, high on the ice cap, to maintain a 24-hour observation of weather conditions throughout the winter. On 11 August Scott's party set off to establish the station.*

Travelling to the ice cap. *They took four sledges, each carrying a weight of 600 pounds and pulled by a team of seven dogs. Often it required all five men to advance one sledge.*

Gruelling conditions. *The 300 yards of tumbled ice was so precipitous and slick that without wearing crampons it was impossible to stand up.*

The weather station. *After 24 days of continual ascent the weather station was finally established at a height of 8,600 feet, 127 miles from Big Flag Depot.*

Christmas at the base hut.
Gino is in the middle, with
Chapman and Gertrude
to the right. Scott sits in
the front row with his pipe.
Meanwhile Courtauld was
alone at the ice cap station
where the temperature was
– 30° C.

Hampton and Courtauld after piling more boxes onto the
flap. We had to turn over by numbers, all facing the same
way at the same time. The wind got even worse. At every big
gust all three of us were lifted right off the ground as the tent
swayed with the wind.

It must have been terrifying but Chapman loved it: in a dangerous
situation, he was steady and in charge. He had always wanted to be
an action hero. His father Frank had been one when *he* was young:
captain of his public school and of the football team. But contrary
to his instincts Frank had become a solicitor – and loathed the job.
A partner with his brother in a family law firm in the Temple, he
had taken to drink and grown negligent.

Chapman was the second of two children. His mother never
recovered from his birth, dying from blood poisoning less than a
month afterwards without ever learning about the disgrace and ruin
that the family faced. The firm's managing clerk had embezzled a
client's funds; responsibility lay with Frank and his brother. Under
threat of prosecution both fled to Canada. 'From the age of two and
a half I was brought up by an elderly parson and his wife,' is how
Chapman describes his childhood.

Every morning and evening we had long family prayers;
each Sunday... my brother and I had to attend Matins and
Evensong and listen to interminable and learned sermons...
It seemed to me there was no possible escape from the flames
of hell, and even now I cannot hear church bells without a
sinking of the heart.

His brother was an amiable but slow-witted boy and from an early
age Chapman learnt to make his own life, wandering alone with
fishing rod, butterfly net and a jam jar for the catch. At eight he was

sent away to a boarding school remote in the Yorkshire moors. The building had been a lunatic asylum and one of the classrooms still had padded walls and a stout door drilled with a peephole. Meanwhile Chapman's dishonoured father achieved his full negative potential by becoming bankrupt. Joining the army as a private soldier at the start of World War I, he was killed on the Somme in 1916 when Chapman was nine. The boy showed his feelings to no one – then, or in his memoirs. He was indomitable. 'I remember boys banging Chapman over the head with cricket bats to see how hard he could take it. This was not bullying, he egged them on. He was proud of his toughness,' a school friend recalls. He learnt to swim by means of the standard technique employed at the time: he was thrown in the deep end and left to fathom the skill for himself. This was his own choice; other coaching methods were available at the school, though they were thought cissy. Even in childhood he was gutsy and bold but there was a further aspect to this characteristic which was noted by a young assistant master: he was 'completely fearless, no regard for danger, but careless too of the safety of others, always doing something to place other lives in jeopardy as well as his own.' The reader may care to recall this youthful assessment when he or she comes to the chapter on Chapman and Courtauld at the ice cap station.

The parson guardian to Chapman and his brother retired. Responsibility for the two boys passed to another elderly vicar and his wife. 'Uncle Sam' was a charming, other-worldly man; 'Aunt Ella' a stern bluestocking, stingy and austere. It seems their marriage was never consummated. 'Mine has been an ugly life,' Sam once wrote to a friend. 'I am sure that in the past you have guessed where the twist was.'

Aged fourteen Chapman was sent to Sedbergh, a public school in the Lake District surrounded by mountains. Its academic record was fair, but it was more fanatical than most in its creed of character-building through cold baths, discipline and games. A further zest was added to this ethos by Sedbergh's particular tradition of spartan endurance – the virtue of the stiff upper lip. One might think Chapman would fit easily into this regimen, but he did not for he could not abide organised games. His stubborn resistance caused him endless trouble but, after being beaten four days in a row for avoiding cricket, his housemaster allowed him to pursue a sport of his own choice: rock climbing.

As with Gino, it was this that provided the epiphany which enabled him to focus the impulse smouldering within him. 'As long as I can remember I have always been fascinated by danger, and at first, I admit, I pursued it for its own sake,' he wrote later. In *Living Dangerously* he analyses the urge that motivated Gino, Scott, himself and others among the explorers. Whatever it was, it was a compulsion, a craving, for it dictated their lives. Whatever it was, it was the only thing that provided satisfaction and allowed them to live in full. It is not fanciful to compare it to a drug, for these are the symptoms of addiction.

In that book Chapman asks: who in this world is really happy? Who really does seem to be enjoying life? He says it is the so-called uncivilised people, 'so long as they are not so primitive as to be obsessed by fear. I am thinking of the Greenland Eskimo, the herdsmen of Tibet and the little aborigines of the Malayan jungle.' What these groups have in common is that 'they spend their time in the open air; their livelihood depends on hunting... and in the process of living they are in conflict with the forces of nature; they are forced by circumstances to face hazards and even to live dangerously.' Chapman says their (and his) happiness derives from four sources: 'a simplification of the objects of life, a degree of companionship, beautiful surroundings – and the element of danger.' But, he reasons, there must be *justification* for the risk. Self-exposure to danger cannot be wanton, it must be undertaken in pursuit of a particular objective. It requires a valid, at best a noble, purpose. The resulting emotional change – or 'high', if one is to continue the drug analogy – comes not from risk itself but from *overcoming fear*. The effect of this is to force all the senses fully open; body and mind are wedded in a state of heightened reality, the user becomes intensely, vividly *aware*. The physiological condition can also be expressed in spiritual terms. As Irenaeus puts it, 'the glory of God is a man fully alive'.

At Sedbergh, Chapman climbed alone; there was no one else on the rope who might save him if he fell. 'I did no rope climbing at that time but some of the descents to ravens' or peregrines' nests... reduced the margin of safety to the slenderest limit. But it was good practice; it gave self-reliance.' Much of his holiday was spent alone: walking rough country while studying it with the eye of a naturalist, watching birds and shooting them. He found no conflict in this, for the birds provided food for the household which justified the excitement of the hunt. 'Frozen finger close on the half-forgotten gun, the body becomes tense as the air is filled with the beat of wings... The gun's flash startles the quiet dawn. There is a thudding splash as a heavy body hits the sodden mud flats. Nothing can be greater than the thrill of one's first goose.' Yet the pleasure he felt was not wholly physical. 'While I was waiting... I learnt, amongst other poems, the whole of Omar Khayyam, Keats' "Ode to a Nightingale", "The Shropshire Lad" and "The Ancient Mariner".'

At fifteen Chapman fell in love with the first of many girlfriends – he was always falling in love. Mary Swainson was the daughter of yet another vicar. He 'never even kissed me. We did, however, have long talks about our emotional and growing up problems... [He] felt his orphanhood very much indeed. He did not get on with his elder brother, who was different from him temperamentally... he felt rootless, and I have often wondered to what extent his lifelong craving for exploration was partly a search for a true home...'

The crowded tent Chapman lay in on the glacier somehow survived the night. At dawn the wind stopped. Riley came over from the base in the motorboat, bringing Arpika and Gertrude who sewed up the damaged tents. The one that had blown away was found in the gorge below the glacier, together with most of the missing equipment. Dressing the dogs in their canvas boots and wearing crampons themselves, the ice cap party and their support group spent the next two days getting the six heavily loaded sledges up the uneven slant of bare ice to the foot of Buggery Bank. There they hammered iron spikes into the ice and used block and tackle to haul the sledges up. A couple of days later they were still doing so. A blizzard blew up that night but next evening the sky was afire with a lurid light over the sea, while in their camp they sat smoking their pipes and watched the pale lasers of the northern lights shimmering in a luminous curtain of ruby, green and gold above the horizon.

By 1 November they had completed winching the sledges to the top of Buggery, but the work was arduous. 'The fine snow gets in everywhere,' Chapman noted, 'fills our pockets, blows down our necks and freezes onto our faces in an icy mass. The snow thaws on one's forehead, runs down and turns to ice on one's eyebrows. My eyes froze up solid...' The supporting party returned to base. The remaining men moved the sledges two at a time through the crevasses while Wager went ahead on a long rope attached to the leading sledge, probing the solidity of the ground. The snow bridges were weak and often his foot went through into the void below. That evening the blizzard blew hard and it was all the six men could do to erect the tent. The wind continued the following day and night without a lull, preventing travel. Next morning all the boxes and sledges were buried beneath the snow and had to be dug out, and several of the dogs had bitten free of their harness. Men and dogs had to haul all day and by evening were bad-tempered and exhausted. 'It looks as if it will be some time before we reach the station,' Chapman wrote.

On 5 November the gale was so bad they lay up all day. Alarmed by the slowness of their advance they were on half rations and their conditions were intensely uncomfortable; their fur sleeping bags were soaking wet as they could not bear to undress before getting into them. The inside of the tent was coated with hoar-frost which fell on them in a shower with each blast of wind. The dogs were already showing signs of weakening, the days were fast shortening and the weather was likely to get worse as winter closed in. They had travelled only ten miles in eleven days. It was clear to Chapman that some of the party must return in order to conserve rations, but who and how many? 'Gale continued with increasing violence all day and night,' Chapman wrote. 'Our tents simply can't last much longer. It is impossible to breathe with this wind. My feet have been numb since yesterday; I can't feel anything when walking on them. In the evening the gale became ghastly. The wind must be well over 100mph. It must have felt rather like this being under shellfire during the war. If the tent goes we are corpses...'

Sharing these appalling conditions and relying upon Chapman's leadership and each other to get through them had brought these six men close. Physically in the cramped tents, but otherwise as well. 'Lying out perhaps for four consecutive days in a blizzard on the ice cap, I learned what my companions really thought about life,' says Chapman. 'I was astonished to find that most of them had disliked school chapel as much as I had and that none of them had any more definite philosophy of life than I had myself.'

For him, both at school and at home, religion had been inescapable. Chapman never overcame his dislike of it. 'I could not reconcile myself... to the Victorian interpretation of God... A religion that tells us all our natural desires are wicked cannot be right.' He could not withhold his contempt for 'singing what seemed to me ridiculous hymns and repeating equally nonsensical prayers.' Yet the clerical influence of childhood proved hard to escape and 'I was more than ever certain that I was damned.' Aunt Ella wrote him the sort of letter he had become used to, and to which he replied: 'Yes, now I am head of the house I do realise the true value of character, and to a certain extent the value of Christ as a friend; but somehow it is awfully hard for a boy, when you seem to get on well without, and everyone else does too.'

Though he had become a member of the school establishment, his non-conformist nature never quite fitted in. A contemporary at Sedbergh remembers him 'displaying at times a pathetic desire to be liked.' He had a generous nature, but he had less money than other boys. He treated them, but more than once was suspected of stealing from them in order to do so. Once at Cambridge money remained a problem despite his scholarship. 'Went to Wordie... he said he heard I didn't pay my bills. I think he'd only heard of the small ones.' He had a tendency to extravagance. 'Ye Gods, I shall be twenty soon. I feel there are a lot of things I wish to do before I am... but I must do more work. My debts at present are more than they should be... I shall give up dancing, it is a waste of money and most people consider it an aid to petting. I will keep off girls much more in future...'

He started to suffer from bouts of depression, which would affect him throughout his life. 'I have not felt quite so miserable for a long time. I really am in a very serious condition. I have no principles, scruples or morals whatsoever, I have bad health as a rule, I have no money, I am getting into debt, worst of all I have no brain... No one realises what an utter rotter and dud I am.' Despite going to the cinema, eating out and dancing, his despair kept recurring. 'I do feel depressed, I hope it will soon pass over... I really shall shoot myself soon.' Forty years later, in just such a state of gloom, he would do so.

Risk and danger could dispel his endemic bleakness, but mountaineering was impossible during term; mountains took too long to reach on the narrow roads of the day in his ancient convertible. But *climbing* was possible and at hand. Nightclimbing, as it was known – scaling the roofs and towers of the college buildings – was a cult at Cambridge in the twenties. Those who practised it did not publicise their achievements; they spoke of their activity only to each other and took it seriously. As it required. Some of the ascents were advanced and perilous. Parties of two or three climbers would rope together to surmount them by moonlight in the early hours, and the downside was certain rustication if they were found out, death if they got it wrong. The nightclimbers were a secret society. Having graduated by his first ascent, Chapman joined it to discover one of its members and leader on the rope was Gino Watkins. In the small world of the university Gino was already somewhat famous for his expeditions to the Arctic. Now, in their shared taste for climbing and the thrill of risk Chapman had found a spirit that matched his own – a blood brother.

'Amazed still to be here. The most fearful night imaginable,' Chapman noted in his diary the day following the gale. 'The wind reached hurricane force... I really thought no tent could possibly stand against it... I don't think Lemon will stand the journey but he has guts... Feet still numb, I wonder if they'll drop off. I wish I had more experience of frostbite so as to know what to expect. I smoked my pipe and read *Tess of the D'Urbervilles*... I wondered how long one could exist in a fur bag before freezing to death.' That afternoon the wind dropped. On going outside the tent Chapman found one of his dogs frozen into the ice by his tail. Thinking it was held only by the tuft of fur at the end, he cut it off – to discover he had sliced through the bone. 'But he seems quite happy,' he noted. Most of the other dogs were limping and looked half-dead. The light was poor and visibility bad. It was vital that they keep on the line of flags, for if they missed them they would lose all hope of finding the station.

By 9 November they had travelled fifteen miles in fifteen days. Men and dogs were suffering from the cold. Chapman lists what he was wearing. Three pairs of socks and three pairs of blanket shoes and fur boots, pants and vest, sweater, blanket trousers and coat, windproof trousers and coat, canvas leggings to keep the snow out, two pairs of wool mitts and wolf-skin mitts, wool helmet and windproof hood. His sleeping bag had half an inch of water inside. 'Things certainly look very black' he observes. Next day he records: '48° of frost in the night [-9°C]. Visibility bad, diffused light and slight snow. Suddenly saw a small moving object in the distance away to the left. A dog? A bear?'

It was Gino and Scott returning exhausted and in poor shape from their southern journey. Both groups hurried to meet each other. 'Where are you going?' asked Gino in alarm. 'Not into the ice cap station? But Good Lord, you'll never get there.'

'Oh I know,' Chapman answered cheerfully. His breezy response broke the tension and both of them laughed. Gino and Scott had had a frightful journey, Chapman noted. Their faces bore witness to what they had gone through; their cheeks and foreheads were blackened by frost, noses and cheekbones flayed raw by the wind. On the last of their food while pinned down by the blizzard they had accepted the fact that they were going to freeze to death. 'They had given up all hope and had morphia tablets ready,' he says.

Standing there in that bleak infinity surrounded by tired men and fifty-four worn-out dogs collapsed in the snow, Chapman explained his own problems to Gino: the poor state of their sledges; how long it had taken to reach this far; how much they had had to consume of the rations intended for the ice cap station, and how little remained. Gino said, 'Never mind about the wireless. Take its weight in food and concentrate entirely on getting in and bringing out Bingham and D'Aeth. You may have to abandon the station. I don't know. You'll just have to use your own judgement and do the best you can.' His instructions were characteristic of his style of leadership. They were *practical*, for only on reaching the station would it be possible to assess the situation – but Chapman found them unsatisfactory. Wager, who was in Chapman's party, said, 'Gino thought we should have great difficulty in making the station and several times said we must abandon it if necessary and eat our dogs.' 'Gino wouldn't help me at all,' wrote Chapman. 'He said he didn't know how things stood and hurried on.'

Next day Chapman dumped the heavy wireless, charging motor, seven boxes of stores, and sent back three of his party, pressing on with Courtauld and Wager. 'We took the three best teams of dogs... also the best of everything they had, sledges, clothes, books, whips. We have arranged a code for the aeroplane. An X in the snow if landing impossible and an O if possible. If there is no sign of us by 10 December they will send out a search party.' That night Courtauld came into Chapman's tent saying he had an idea. He said he felt that he had contributed little to the expedition so far, and would like to remain alone at the ice cap station. He told Chapman what he knew already: that at this rate of travel they were going to take so long to reach the station there would not be enough food remaining to supply two men there throughout the winter. He said he hated Wager, and vice-versa, and couldn't stand the idea of sharing a tent with him. He stressed (falsely) that he was used to being alone, insisting he knew his own mind and wanted to man the station by himself. Chapman heard him out and said they would discuss it when they had got to the station.

They pushed on. The blizzards continued; they were pinned

down for two or three days at a time. The dogs were recalcitrant as ever. 'It's just amazing what one can do to these dogs under such conditions. One behaves like an animal and hits them anywhere with any weapon,' Chapman writes. They advanced a further two miles in two days. It looked to him as though they would have to go on until the dog food was finished, then kill off the weaker dogs as food for the others. When and if they found the station they would have to man-haul the sledges home. On 20 November he records:

Worst day I've ever had. Several times I just couldn't go on... 21 November. Only a few hours daylight now. My sleeping-bag was frozen solid in a rolled-up position; all we could do to straighten it out tonight. 23 November. Ears, nose and fingers frost-bitten today. A bitch in Courtauld's team had a puppy. We relentlessly fed it to another team, and the same with three other puppies. Yet the bitch pulled well between each. Poor brute, but what else could we do. 25 November. Sleeping-bags absolutely sodden. Toes and fingertips rotting slowly. I thought a lot about good old Westmorland today and Sedbergh. It's odd to think of life going on just the same there. And us poor shits slaving our silly souls out here – and why? God knows, but it's bloody good fun really.

At last, after travelling for thirty-nine days, they reached their destination. 'We missed the last few flags but stopped when our sledge-wheel told us that we had gone far enough... I found the station a hundred yards to the left. It was 8 p.m., four hours after sunset. The others would hardly believe me... then we walked into the yard and down the tunnel shouting, "Evening Standard!" Evening Standard!" God knows they were glad to see us! We were five weeks overdue.'

That night all of them packed into the station's tent and slept until 10 a.m. next morning. Outside it was blowing a furious gale, but they knew they must start back for base the following day. In the evening Chapman cooked up a premature Christmas dinner with treats they had brought up for that purpose.

MENU
Game Soup
Sardines in Olive Oil
Ptarmigan
Plum Pudding
Rum Sauce (very)
Angels on Sledges
Dessert (Dates and Raisins)
Mincemeat, Jam, Hot Grog, Tea (with milk)

They discussed what to do. There was not enough food to last two people until the station could be relieved in spring, and it might prove impossible to resupply them by aeroplane. But to abandon it meant the failure of the Air-Route Expedition. Their survey work – both that already completed and what was planned for next year – was valueless without a record of weather conditions on the ice cap. Without knowledge of its blizzards and extremes of temperature and wind speed no aircraft of the period could attempt to overfly the area in a passenger service. Now an airline can fly *above* the weather, but then the frail machines in existence would be blown out of the sky or literally torn apart by hurricane-force winds.

The choice facing Chapman as leader of the relief party was stark. Either they must close down the station, or one man must remain there alone. Courtauld was keen to do so. He claimed he was used to solitude (though this was not the case 'except perhaps in his own head,' as Scott observed later). He would have work to occupy him, plenty of books, and tobacco. What Courtauld did not voice, but was known to everyone, was that he detested Wager. He found him fussy, quick-tempered and rude, and believed Wager reciprocated his dislike. But there was a further and more profound reason why Courtauld wanted to stay which he confided only to his diary. He thought his role in the Expedition, and in life, had been insignificant. He wanted *'to do something big'*.

Wager was dead against the idea; he felt it reflected adversely on himself. Bingham and D'Aeth, who had spent the last two months at the station, also opposed it. One day Bingham had been out alone when the Union Jack by the tent flapped loudly. Panicked by the noise, he had rushed back inside in terror. D'Aeth had experienced the same paranoia. While reading the instruments outside he had caught sight of the screen protecting the thermometers. Mistaking it for a strange man, he had bolted down the tunnel like a scared rabbit.

It was Chapman's call: abort the mission or agree to Courtauld's staying? Eventually he gave in, but he was uneasy. 'He knows his own mind I suppose,' he wrote in his diary. 'It's a marvellous effort and I hope to God he gets away with it.' Next morning Courtauld made breakfast for the others before they left. They set off at 5 a.m. The ice field, covered by an unmarked counterpane of snow, stretched away to an infinite horizon in the blanched light of a low moon. The temperature was -8°C. 'It was bitterly cold and I didn't watch them long,' he wrote. 'Coming out an hour later I could just see them as a speck in the distance. Now I am quite alone. Not a dog or even a mosquito to look at.'

Chapman had left Courtauld with enough food and fuel to last until April, taking only half-rations for eight days for his own party. It was not enough to make it back to base, but there was a solution. 'Next day I killed Bruno and cut him up.' Their journey home was ghastly. Men and dogs were exhausted, the party's candles ran out, the paraffin was finished so they could not cook or warm the tent, their sleeping bags were sopping wet. All that remained for men and beasts to eat was margarine. The days were so short now they travelled in murky twilight or, when the clouds cleared, by the gleam of the moon. D'Aeth was suffering badly from frostbite and could not work. His morale crumbled and he lagged behind the rest. One night when they made camp he failed to appear. Although exhausted, Chapman trekked back to find him stumbling in the wrong direction, and saved his life. It took them over two weeks to get back. On the descent of Buggery Bank Chapman's sledge crashed and one of the runners broke off. A few yards further Bingham's struck an ice shelf and disintegrated into debris.

On the first day that flying was possible after weeks of foul weather, Gino flew in search of them and spotted the party coming down Buggery. Landing back at base, he harnessed his dogs and sledged across the fjord with the Eskimo girls to meet them at the foot of the glacier. 'He was more than relieved to see us all safe,' says Courtauld. 'Of course they all thought us dead. Gertrude frightfully glad to see me.'

Meanwhile, 130 miles distant and 8,500 feet high on the ice cap, the temperature had gone down to -15°C, twenty-four-hour night had shut in, and Courtauld was beginning his third week alone.

Sexual Selection

At base camp Gino and his party made ready for darkness and the long night of Arctic winter. Public school had prepared them for communal living but it was another model that he had in mind while making his arrangements for the coming experience.

Although none in the party were rich – except Courtauld, who was absent – all had experience of traditional country house living, if only as guests, and this was the archetype Gino followed. Throughout childhood and adolescence the Watkins family (and Nanny) had spent Christmas and school holidays with their Monsell cousins at Dumbleton Hall in the Vale of Evesham. This was not one of the great houses like Wilton or Longleat which for generations has been home to an aristocratic line of courtiers, statesmen, patrons, eccentrics or drunks who have inscribed or lurched their way through the pages of English history, bearing a name still resonant to this day. Dumbleton, with only twenty bedrooms, was modest by comparison. Yet the mock-baronial pile was surrounded by lawn and park; the estate included a lake, church, cricket ground and its own dairy farm. The house was set in a gently rolling landscape of fields and woods: the English countryside at its pastoral best. The place belonged to Gino's Uncle Bobby (his mother's brother), the impoverished son of an Anglo-Irish rector whose hymns are still sung in Anglican churches to this day. Although without capital or much in the way of education, Bobbie possessed worldly skills, advancing from midshipman to First Lord of the Admiralty; in the course of this progress he had married money in the tall, shy, awkward shape of Aunt Sybil, only daughter of the Birmingham industrialist who had invented the zip fastener.

Despite Dumbleton's quaintly grand exterior, the house was not equipped or run for show. It was a functional family home, spacious and comfortable, furnished for living, for family, dogs, horses, weekend guests and the pleasures of civilised life. Though children and servants necessarily formed part of this scene they inhabited their own quarters, fulfilling discrete yet harmonious roles. Despite its scale, Dumbleton – and similar country houses of the period – provided in their own manner a model of orderly simplicity. Nothing was permitted to disturb the comforting impression that here, if perhaps not everywhere, God was in his heaven, all was right with the world.

How to achieve such an idyll of exploitative perfection was a subject covered by several handbooks in print at the time, most notably *Mrs Beeton's Guide to Household Management and the Handling of Domestic Staff*.

In the base hut, which resembles a boys' dormitory in a disorderly school from which matron has run off with the headmaster, its period tone suggesting *Brideshead-on-Ice*, the Eskimo girl, Tina, gathers up the greasy plates from the dinner table, as she has been taught. Piling on top of these the pots and pans in which the meal has been cooked, she carries the teetering stack over to the sealed window. Balancing the heap on her knee and steadying it with one hand, she uses the other to undo the latch and pries the window open only long enough to chuck the lot out into the snow for the dogs to lick clean. Arpica, the second Eskimo girl, appears to be off duty at this moment for she is watching the kitchen maid's activity from where she lies sprawled indolently across Gino's knees, while the third, Gertrude, rises to pad across the hut in her sealskin boots to put another record on the gramophone and wind it up before returning to sit on Chapman's lap.

> Button up your overcoat
> When the wind is free
> Take good care of yourself
> You belong to me.

Above the hiss of the needle on the bakelite disc, the hit tune of the previous spring blares scratchily in the crowded hut. The place is an untidy hovel of bunks and equipment, draped with clothes drying in the stove's warmth. The atmosphere is dense and humid, a close, comforting fog of tobacco smoke, cooking smells and body smells. For the first time since many weeks all the explorers are reunited and living together. Except for Courtauld, alone without a radio on the ice cap station, where the temperature is -40°C and endless night surrounds him.

Chapman as leader of that party had hated the responsibility of leaving him there, though he would have hated even more to be the man responsible for the failure of the expedition by abandoning the station. And Courtauld had *volunteered* to remain alone, indeed had appeared strangely keen to do so. If Gino felt anxiety about Courtauld's situation he did not show it. Even if he thought Chapman had made the wrong call he could hardly say so. He'd made him leader of the mission and given him a free hand.

At base the days were very brief now; most of the time dusk covered the earth and sea. On the rare clear morning an orange red disc crept above the horizon at 11 a.m. to flare violet, purple and sparkling green across the pack ice and pinnacles of the bergs, move sideways and sink in liquid fire, returning the world to twilight. Yet, if weather permitted and the moon was full, Gino intended to fly into the station to drop supplies – though not the wireless set which had been buried by Chapman near Big Flag and could not be found. A hangar to shelter the two Gypsy Moths had now been completed. The *Quest* had delivered the forgotten ski undercarriages from Iceland – departing immediately before she was frozen in – and these had been fitted to one of the aircraft, though it could not take off until the ice on the fjord had frozen thick enough to bear its weight. Darkness provided no opportunity for surveying, but there was work to be done. Apart from sledging rations, Gino deliberately had brought very little food for humans and dogs, and by now there were sixty animals to feed, plus thirteen men. So he took a party up to the lake and blasted a hole through the ice with dynamite. It was the sort of fishing which appealed to him, 'No rot about being sporting,' as Scott noted. Others looked for seals in the fjord.

The living room of the hut all of them shared was 20 feet by 12 feet. To enter it they had to pass through the wireless room/workshop, then the kitchen. Lined by double-tiered bunks, the room was so narrow you could not walk through it while people were seated at the central table. Personal possessions were kept heaped on their bunks during the day then heaved out onto the floor at night; there was no storage space except for the loft, one end of which had been appropriated by the Eskimo staff.

The three Eskimo girls cleaned the hut, prepared and served meals, and washed up by throwing the tin crockery to the dogs as we have seen. 'They were quite hurt when told to wash them again,' says Chapman. 'However... later on we were not nearly so fussy.' The staff proved quite incapable of remembering anything from one day to the next. The kitchen stove had to be relit six or seven times each morning, while coal and water were invariably 'perangera' – an expressive word meaning 'there isn't any'.

The girls performed these duties – and more – in return for cigarettes and being allowed to play the gramophone. Which they did incessantly, grinding down their favourite records until they were only noise. Driven mad by the constant repetition of *Spread a Little Happiness as You Go By* one of the explorers flung the record out the window and broke it. Arpika sewed the pieces together again, but it wasn't the same afterwards.

After dinner the men played cards or roulette at the table, or lay on their bunks to read. Gino and Chapman passed most evenings in the loft with the girls. But the hut was shanty-built; you could hear everything taking place in it and some of the group were distinctly uncomfortable with the arrangement and the sounds coming through the thin ceiling. One of them, Martin Lindsay, grumpily notes in his diary, 'The female servants of an Expedition should be as prescribed for bed-makers in an old university statute, *horrida et senex* – ugly and old.'

Despite the sexual resentment, or perhaps envy, the members of the expedition got on well. 'It was amazing how little we quarrelled,' Chapman remarks. Most of them had never met before the expedition started, yet here they were spending nearly twenty hours out of the twenty-four in a hut about the size of a large room. Among them were men who had seen ten years' service in the Army, Navy and Air Force, while others were fresh from Cambridge. They did not appear to have much in common yet they had hardly any quarrels. The average age was very much younger than that of any other expedition: that, perhaps, was their saving grace.

'As quietly as if it had been a Scottish shooting-party, Gino had organised the greatest British Expedition to the Arctic for half a century, and he was carrying it through in the same unofficial, unheroic spirit,' Scott wrote later. He was in awe of Gino. He did not make friends easily and those friendships he *had* formed at Cambridge were with rugger buggers and hearties very unlike Gino. Aspects of his leader still troubled him; he didn't know what to make of his irreverence and attitude to authority, he had no respect for obvious effort, he thought keenness and striving 'hot-making', he dressed like a fop and mocked organised sport, which Scott excelled in. Gino adored jazz and dancing, while he himself was lead-footed, and hated dancing. The two men could scarcely have been more different yet they were close. In Labrador they had grown to know each other – or rather, as Scott says, he had got to know a *side* of Gino. And after their return Gino had taken Scott, a newcomer to London, under the wing of his own makeshift family. He had encouraged a friendship with his sister Pam, taken him with them to dances and to nightclubs, invited him to Davos. Gino had been extraordinarily generous to him – something Scott was unused to. Metropolitan life and this social milieu were new to him, he was no sophisticate. He owned a dinner jacket and had learned which fork to use but conversation, particularly with women, came hard to him. He was envious of Gino's ease and wit, how he snapped his fingers at convention, the way he appeared to sail so effortlessly through life.

Arctic winter had clamped down on the base. On 12 December the sun failed to rise and would not be seen again until it peeped above the southern horizon on 11 January. Evenings in the hut they shared were long and Scott had time to observe Gino and the way he ran the house party. 'His method of leadership was entirely his own,' he notes. The President of the Royal Geographical Society wrote of him later, 'Gino Watkins was destined to command... Leadership came to him naturally.' *How so?* one wonders. It is said that in order to command one must first learn to obey, but Gino never had; he was an instinctive seditionary. Scott says it was because Gino never had occupied any place *but* that of leader, so had to serve his apprenticeship simultaneously. In rock climbing he was a leader from the first because his temperament made him so; but he was never afraid to ask advice, while, in gatherings of mountaineers he listened instead of talking so that he quickly learned all that he should know. When he sailed for Edge Island he had no first-hand knowledge of the conditions. He was successful because he could sum up positions quickly and act without hesitation, and he was a tactful and popular leader because he asked the opinions of the members of the party who had each some special knowledge to impart. In Labrador it had been the same. Everyone he came in contact with was gratified by his respectful interest in all they said and, without fully realising it, they did what he wanted them to do.

The eccentricity of this method of leadership was reflected in the names people called each other. All were known by their surnames – but Gino was always 'Gino'. That alone cramped the possibilities of service discipline, says Scott. 'Besides he gave himself no privileges at all. His bed was no more comfortable than ours: probably it was less so, judging by the dog harness and rifles which were piled on top of it. His clothes were no better and his private possessions far less numerous. His dogs I had given to him after selecting what I considered the best team for myself. Only his native hunting instruments were superior because he had taken great trouble in acquiring them. I was reminded that once in Labrador I heard a man call him "Boss", and Gino had been a little embarrassed and very much amused.' At first there had been some unease about this absence of discipline. One or two of the Service men in particular were upset by the apparently casual suggestions which passed for commands; they would have appreciated the comfortable definiteness of written orders. Others, although they could not have admitted it, had looked for something more in exploration: a consciousness of adventure and romance. All this was so straightforward and matter-of-fact to the point that if one so much as grew a beard one felt theatrical. Gino's plans and his rebellious 'why-not?' point of view were exciting enough if one could swallow them; but... could anyone so casual have taken the trouble to prepare sufficiently and select the best equipment?

Scott says that Gino's tactic of leadership was to train *each man* to be a leader: his ideal exploring party consisted of nothing else. 'In Gino's opinion, initiative and self-confidence were all important... We were infected by our leader's glorious, self-reliant impudence. Anything might be possible and in any case it was amusing to try.'

In the bleak midwinter frosty wind made moan
Earth stood hard as iron, water like a stone
Snow had fallen, snow on snow, snow on snow
In the bleak midwinter, long ago.

On Christmas Eve the explorers sang carols then unearthed their presents from the loft. Scott celebrated Christmas morning by running naked in the snow, returning to share a special breakfast of sausages and tomatoes. Then they opened the gift-wrapped parcels that had come with them on the *Quest*, the most rewarding of which was a mystery box from one of their Cambridge tutors containing hardback novels, treats to eat, and a selection of new gramophone records which played without cease throughout the rest of that day.

Eskimos value steam as a sign of wealth. The crowded hut was a fog of humidity and tobacco smoke; it was an atmosphere which these fit, clean-living, open-window-in-the-night young men had come to appreciate. In its murky balm they sat down that evening to a dinner of hare soup, tongue, asparagus, baby poussins and Christmas pudding. Heavy though the meal was, following it they held a dance lasting until 2 a.m., with the Eskimo girls partnering all and everyone happy in the seasonal smog of home-sweet-home.

Meanwhile on this Christmas night, alone on the ice cap, Courtauld, who had not seen daylight for two weeks, was writing in his diary:

How jolly to be at home or even at the base. I suppose they will be having a blind and finishing the last of the alcohol. However I haven't done so badly. Excellent porridge for breakfast... and a dinner of rice, honey (made from sugar and margarine), toffee and chocolate. Mollie's pipe going v.g. Book's good... and nothing to disturb the peace except the wind whistling up to an increasing gale and the house which is making rather frightening cracks and thumps. Hope it isn't going to fall in...

Do What is Customary

THE COUNTRY HOUSE shooting-party was a convention of the twenties and thirties. It furnished the setting for several of the plays and movies of those between-the-war years. For those aged over twenty-five or so it included couples, bachelors and single women among the guests; for younger men it provided an extension to university life. A group of undergraduates would gather to pass several days in a large country house, passing their time fishing and shooting. The more remote and wild the area the better. The role of the host was to keep his guests entertained: to supply food, drink and manly sports.

To celebrate New Year's eve 1930/31, Gino suggested some of the explorers might like to spend it with the Eskimos. 'Perhaps they'll invite us to stay with them for the weekend,' he said. Though frivolously expressed, his motive was not entirely social; a serious intention lay behind it. When the expedition had sailed from England they had brought with them cases of the highly concentrated sledging rations Gino had devised, but otherwise the base supplies consisted only of staples. It had always been his plan to live off the land and sea while in the Arctic. On 30 December he took Chapman, Riley, Rymill and two dog teams to go visit the larger Eskimo settlement twenty miles down the coast to learn to hunt bear and seals. They had two tents with them and could sleep out if necessary, for they were not entirely sure how they would be received.

Their journey, most of it across the smooth surface of frozen-over fjords, was made in one day by moonlight. The whole population of the settlement saw them approaching and turned out to greet them with strange wails of delight. Their big Nansen sledges, the powerful west coast dogs pulling in single trace as they had now been taught, their clothes, zip-fasteners and skis, everything about the visitors was new and strange. They were warmly received into the winter house which resembled a rancid stable where forty-three people were already living. The occupants shifted over to make room on the communal sleeping bench and they settled down comfortably in the welcoming fug of dogs, children, urine, rotten seal-meat and home cooking.

Their traditional upbringing had made the young explorers rather reserved. Uptight young Englishmen, they were initially somewhat set aback by the way the Eskimo women pounced upon them to undress them. But that same upbringing had also taught them the prime rule of good manners: *Do what is customary.* 'The winter house is kept so warm the natives usually wear nothing except a small loin-cloth and we naturally followed their example,' Chapman explains.

Conversation was difficult, for they had learnt only a rather basic vocabulary from the girls in the loft, but after dinner of a huge plateful of boiled seal and a tin of snow-water they retired to bed with the rest on the sleeping platform, which was so crowded a further four bodies made little difference. The dormitory hut was tightly sealed. There was no ventilation and no fresh air at all, and once they had put out their pipes the heat and stench were suffocating. The night was raucous with crying babies and at one point interrupted by a violent dogfight in the middle of the floor which sent everything flying. Yet they slept well and when they woke next day it would be to find that the smell had so much become a part of them they hardly noticed it.

There is no dawn. Beneath the light of the moon the winter house resembles a giant snow-covered molehill, organic to the coast of the fjord. Within its noxious interior the woman is the first to wake. A dark, wrinkled face with dirty yellow eyes emerges from the mass of furs heaped on the sleeping-platform. At forty she is already old. Seated on the platform's edge she draws on her foxskin trousers then, holding them up with one hand, waddles across the floor to squat over the sliced-open two-gallon can that serves as a urinal. Returning to the platform, she pulls on the long white boots which have been her pillow and goes to cut up some sealmeat. Feeding the oil lamp with a lump of fat, she uses a splinter of root to separate the floating wicks, teasing their flicker into a guttering flame.

Shadows leap and flutter around the walls of the winer house. The hump of piled furs spread across the sleeping platform stirs with movement as figures crawl from it into the bleary light and stumble towards the urinal; the accumulated odours of the night waft free to enrich the atmosphere of the sealed hut. A ripe fart vents into the air, mingling with the smell of sweat, piss, foul breath and cooking. The explorers wriggle out of their sleeping bags and dress while the Eskimos surrounding them sit up to cough and hawk up phlegm. One man blows his nose into his hand and then swallows the gob of greenish mucus at a gulp. Another clears his throat with a hoarse rasp and spits a clotted cord of goo in a high arc to land in the communal spittoon by the pile of seal meat.

Deciding to skip breakfast for the moment, Gino and the three

Europeans go outside to rouse and harness up their dogs, buckling the frozen braces with chilly fingers. By the time the Eskimo hunters come out to do likewise they are ready. The night is windless, clear and bright with stars. Returning into the foul murk of the winter house only long enough to collect their rifles, the young men whip up their two teams and follow the hunters' sledges onto the surface of the frozen fjord into an immense, spectral, black-and-white world spread out beneath the light of the moon.

The seal was the basis of the whole of Eskimo culture. No vegetables or cereal crops grow in the Arctic and the only fruit to be found during two months in summer are sparse bushes of whortleberries sprouting between the rocks. The seal's meat and blubber provided 98 per cent of an Eskimos' diet. The fresh blood was drained off and frozen; every part of the animal was eaten except the hide, flippers, bones, lining to the lungs, and the anus. Meat and liver provided the best eating but the contents of the stomach were also consumed, as were the intestines which were squeezed clean of excrement between the fingers then boiled and filled with fat to create a delicacy. The layer of rich blubber just beneath the hide was reserved for children, who for a treat were sometimes given the eyes to munch. Lice were a prized snack. The skin of the seal gave the Eskimo people their clothing; with the hair removed it was waterproof at sea. The larger bearded seal and savage bladder-nosed seal – both of which were dangerous to hunt – provided hull covering for kayaks and umiaks. Their teeth were made into toggles, fish hooks and hunting gear.

For the Eskimo, hunting was the remorseless purpose of life. Everything and life itself depended on the hunt. The system of communism on which survival rested was nowhere more evident than in this principal activity. An Eskimo did not say, 'I am going out to kill a seal', but 'I am going out to get my share of seal'. The manner in which food was distributed after a hunt is telling: first the dogs were fed, then the children, then the hunters, lastly the women. The way the kill was divided up between everyone made individual hoarding impossible. There were no degrees of wealth; all were hungry, or all gorged and were replete.

They were a tribe and acted and thought as a tribe. Individual roles within the organisation seemed archetypal: hunter, woman, child. No one's lifestyle differed substantially from another's. No one saved, no hunter accumulated food or goods for his family or himself. Eskimo people never ate alone, but tended to share everything. Education and schools as we known them were non-existent. Whatever impinged on material existence was of great interest; zip fasteners intrigued them, but they seemed to have little curiosity about life outside their own icy world and few aspirations beyond the success of the hunt. Hunting was everything; they did not much care for any idea that did not relate to it.

In summer when the pack ice broke up and open water appeared between the floes, seals were hunted by kayak, but now when Gino and the others were staying with the settlement the surface of the fjord was frozen solid. Yet seals are warm-blooded mammals who must breathe, which they do in the crack of water which friction produces between the hull of an iceberg and the surrounding pack ice, and at breathing holes they keep open in the ice. These holes are very difficult to locate. Only polar bears find them easily through their acute sense of smell, and the reason the explorers carried rifles was in case they met with these, their contenders and aggressive rivals in the same sport.

Having identified a breathing hole, an Eskimo would sit on a small wooden stool beside it, harpoon in hand... and wait. Often for days without result. It was the longest, coldest, most boring wait imaginable but while doing so for 10,000 years the Eskimo had learnt patience. Over the course of the next few days Gino and the other explorers sat for frozen hours by likely looking holes with zero success, without even the glimpse of a seal.

Another method practised by the Eskimos held greater appeal to them. Two holes were cut in the ice. A hunter stood above one with a long-shafted harpoon. A second man lay prostrate on the ice peering into the other hole, his head and the hole covered by a skin. Moonlight glancing through the ice palely illuminated the underwater world below. Beneath the hunter's hole small ivory lures dangling from his poised harpoon danced and flickered in the water to attract the seal's attention. As it swam within range small movements of the observer's hand directed the hunter's aim, signalling when to strike.

The Eskimos' long harpoons were all in use and unavailable for the Europeans to practise the method, so they attempted to shoot seals from the shore in the tide crack of open water between land and sea. When the head of one appeared, they tried to attract it closer by singing or playing the mouth organ, for seals are inquisitive; the hunter outstretched at his observation hole also twitters and sings to lure them to their death.

Gino and Chapman were both fine shots and succeeded in killing several seals while lodging with the Eskimos, but the problem was recovery and they lost most of them. When hunting they should have a boat available, they realised. Better yet, Gino resolved that they must learn to use kayaks.

In the middle of January the explorers' stay at the Eskimo settlement was interrupted by Scott's unexpected appearance with very bad news. He had come the twenty miles from base in the dark on skis, carrying neither tent nor sleeping bag and trusting to complete the trip without the weather going bad on him. A somewhat casual approach, for if it had, and he had been forced to hole up for any length of time, he would have died of exposure.

He told Gino that on New Year's eve Cozens had flown the seaplane to Angmagssalik to pick up the settlement's radio operator and bring him to stay for the night. The Danish radio operator and Lemon, the base operator, had become friends in the course of their daily morse exchanges and that night those in the hut had given a dinner party at which the two men conversed by tapping on their plates with their knives and forks. After the meal they had managed to tune into the BBC midnight broadcast to hear themselves wished 'a happy New Year to the British Arctic Air-Route Expedition who are spending a year in Greenland's icy mountains.' After which, fuelled on medicinal brandy, they had all gone out on a moonlight skiing party. Next day Cozens had flown the Dane back to Angmagssalik, remaining there overnight. In the meantime a storm blew up. The seaplane broke free of its moorings to be cast up on the shore, and in Cozen's opinion was smashed beyond repair.

The news was deeply disappointing. A key element of the proposal Gino had presented to the RGS – and on which he had obtained his funding – was a flight next spring with both aircraft across the ice cap to Disko Island (now the site of an immense US strategic airbase), continuing to Baffin Land. Then along the shore of Hudson Bay, following the course of the planned air route to Winnipeg, and back again to east Greenland. Now that looked impossible – and, even more worrying, it left only one airplane for the relief or resupply of Courtauld at the ice cap station.

Leaving his group with the Eskimos hunting food to supply the expedition for the winter, Gino and Scott skied back to base. There they picked up Hampton the mechanic, loaded his tools and a wide selection of spare parts into the unreliable motorboat, and sailed to Angmagssalik to examine the seaplane. The damage was extensive. One wing was smashed to matchwood, the other badly crumpled; the tail had been carried away and the longiron twisted. Hampton told Gino he thought he could mend it. Assisted by the resourceful

Rymill, who could turn his hand to anything, he did so. The two men worked fifteen hours a day and it took them six weeks, until March, to complete the job. Hampton later became a BOAC pilot. Scott remarks, 'I wonder if any of his passengers knew that he had once passed as airworthy a Moth with a tail made from the root stump of a Siberian pine that had drifted over the North Pole to Angmagssalik, the carpentry covered with the stuff Eskimo women used for blouses.'

Button up your overcoat, when the wind is free... At base, winter howled down from the ice cap upon the explorers in full fury. Everything not lashed down, whatever its weight, was picked up and flung into the ocean. The hut shook and jumped under the stout wire cables anchoring it to the rocks. Wager, lying flat and clinging to the ground to prevent being swept away, saw the whirling anemometer record 130mph before it lifted off and flew away into the clouds.

In London, before the explorers had signed on for the expedition, Gino had briefed them on what to expect from winter. But those had been mere words uttered in a warm room, spoken by a man who had no experience of conditions here. The reality was awesome, overwhelming. And the weather would be even worse 8,500 feet up on the ice cap, they knew. Courtauld still had enough food, he did not face starvation. But there were other dangers. Cold numbs the brain, and in a blizzard visibility is reduced to inches before your face. In the wind and tumult of the storm he might become confused and lost even within a few yards of the tent, while reading the instruments. He could get stuck in the tunnel, or poison himself with carbon monoxide as Scott had done.

And there was another fouler fear, the worse because it was not named. They knew themselves how aggressive, how horrible the winds were. The storms were a bombardment, an assault on the frail shelter protecting them, a sustained battering on the nerves and mind, which reeled under the relentless cannonade. They were enduring it together, *but what must it be like to suffer it alone?* The Eskimos believed white devils whirled and shrieked within the blizzards, but what vile monsters might solitude give birth to? Unadmitted and undiscussed, at the back of all their minds crouched the horror that Courtauld would go mad.

Conversation in the base hut increasingly centred on when it would be possible to relieve him. Before leaving him at the ice cap station Chapman had agreed a code of noughts or crosses in the snow to indicate whether or not the surface was suitable for a ski plane to land. The sun reappeared in mid January; granted a fine day, an aircraft could make the round trip to the station in three hours. On 8 February the morning dawned clear; the barometer was high and weather looked promising. Everyone at the base gathered on the shore to build a gangway with blocks of ice across the tide-crack which lay between the aircraft shed and the frozen surface of the fjord. The plane's tailskid was supported on a sledge and the aircraft pushed cautiously across the gap.

The Gypsy Moth took off, but halfway to the ice-station met with such heavy cloud it had to turn back. The weather did not permit another attempt until the 25 February when Scott and Cozens took off with a sack of provisions tied beneath the undercarriage. 'It was unbelievably cold in the open cockpit,' says Scott. 'Goodness knows where we got to, certainly not to the station. We did not even see any flags. At one stage the aircraft was almost stationary against the wind.' When landing back at base the plane hit an ice hummock. The undercarriage was smashed and driven through the fuselage. Hampton said it would take a month to repair, and he still had three weeks' work to do on the other plane. Both aircraft were now useless.

When Courtauld was left alone at the ice station, Gino sent

a wireless transmission to his family in England explaining the situation. But that had been at the start of December, it was now the end of February. The Courtauld family had a stake in the expedition – its part-funding and, more vitally, a son. And that son had been alone on the ice cap for three months. *Why had he not been relieved?* Morse messages received at the base from home were increasingly anxious, increasingly insistent.

The storms were now continuous, day after day of wind-whipped cloud and driving snow. The weather showed no sign of abating. One morning while Scott was outside the base hut yet again digging out ration boxes buried by the snow, Gino came up to him. 'I'm afraid someone will have to go and fetch Courtauld while the weather is still bad,' he said. 'I'd like it to be you...'

On the Ice Cap

To *FIND* Courtauld, a single man alone in a small tent perched high on the spine of the ice cap in that shifting desolation of gales and driven snow, would be a precise, difficult operation. And in this weather the journey there – wherever *there* was – with the blizzard howling down the slope into the faces of the men and dogs searching for him, would be very demanding physically. But because of the urgency of the situation someone must make the attempt at once, while the gales were still raging. 'I'd like it to be you,' Gino said to Scott, 'because you know the most about winter travel.'

'I don't think I was taken in,' Scott writes. 'I knew I had to do it yet felt bound to point out my limitations. This was not a case of travelling hopefully, even doggedly. I *had* to arrive.' He had to reach a precise spot in an unchartered featureless desert, although he was unequipped with the range of skills in astronomical observation necessary to do so exactly. He was capable of establishing a latitude, which is effected by measuring the height of the sun at noon, but he had never executed a longitude – a much more complex calculation that depends upon the difference in local time from the meridian at Greenwich. The expedition possessed radio time-signal sets which could be employed to check their half-chronometer watches, but he had never used either sextant or theodolite. Therefore, in searching for Courtauld he decided to employ the old sea captains' method: aim to one side of the station – in this case to the east – and when he found himself on the latitude turn west along it. This was an old-fashioned and laborious technique but Gino approved it, repeating that Scott was the best man for the job. 'I have often tried to fathom Gino's reasoning in picking on me...' he wrote. 'I might have been the most experienced cold weather traveller but I was not by a long way the best fitted to find an exact spot.'

Gino envisaged two possible scenarios. If Courtauld was alive, the station should be visible from a mile away, as it had been when Chapman's party left it. If he were dead, the neglected station would be obliterated by snow and take months to locate. Scott asked Gino what to do when he reached the station. 'I don't think you'll have to abandon it,' he said, 'though, of course, you must use your own judgement about that. We could only afford to have one man there. I don't want you to stay there yourself if the journey home looks difficult. But if it looks easy to get home and the prospect of staying seems unpleasant – well, I'd rather you stayed yourself and sent the others back.'

'Thenceforward it was my show entirely,' says Scott. For the sake of mobility he decided to take only one companion, Riley, and to do without a time-signal set in order to save weight. They left the base on 1 March. The next day they were back, one sledge having broken in half on the glacier. Scott asked for another man so that the loads could be redistributed over three sledges. Lindsay was busy helping Stephenson collect equipment for a journey north to survey the unknown mountains spotted from the seaplane six months before. Gino casually went up to him with, 'I say Lindsay, do you mind going with Scott to relieve Courtauld?' Lindsay said, 'Alright,' and they started off again with their three sledges carrying only equipment and personal kit so they would be easier to manhandle up Buggery Bank and the flagged route through the crevasses to Big Flag, where they could load up with food and supplies. The weather was perfect; they took with them only 'a spot of lunch' to last them to the depot.

A couple of miles short of Big Flag they were blinded by a blizzard. Visibility was down to a few yards. It was impossible to find their way forward so they put up the tent and huddled inside for three days living on the packet of biscuits they had with them, nothing to drink except snow melted over a candle. Then by compass and on snowshoes they waded downwind through eighteen inches of new snow to the coast and found their way back to the base late at night.

On the third attempt they got right away. Climbing the glacier they loaded the sledges at Big Flag, then headed west across the ice cap following the line of flags by compass. Except that they saw no flags at all. Either these had been carried off by the wind, or buried, or they were advancing on the wrong line. To travel on a precise course was vital. The men carried the compasses cradled inside their double gloves to keep their liquid from freezing, but in temperatures of -40°C (by day, and lower at night) the needles became sluggish and took a full minute to find North. The mercury in Scott's sextant froze and ceased to reflect. Once when he had scraped off the ice he peered through it to see not the sun but what he took to be the pitted surface of the moon, only to realise it was his own frozen chin.

Gordon Hayes in *The Conquest of the North Pole* later judged this journey from their meteorological records to be one on which 'the conditions approached the limit of human endurance.' But Scott had been brought up in the stoic code by the austere Protestant relatives who had raised him on Mull, and at boarding school. Whatever the challenge, he had taught himself to endure it and come through. He was tough, both physically and emotionally. When he was a new boy at Fettes and in the sanatorium with measles, his housemaster had walked in to say, "Fraid I've got some bad news, Scott. Cable from Egypt – your father's dead. Don't want you to blub or be silly about it though, you must be a man.'

No one saw Scott blub, ever. His stamina, strength and skill at sport stood him in good stead at school. He became captain of the First XV and First XI. At Cambridge he played for the university and gained his Blue. Lead-footed and uncertain in a ballroom, in the physical world he was entirely sure of himself. Sporting success was held in enormous esteem at that period, both in public school and university. Scott was a hero, his status immeasurable. It didn't help him become anymore at ease socially but throughout his youth he had become accustomed to doing what was required and delivering the goods. He was used to winning.

After seventeen days sledging across the ice cap in appalling conditions or immobilised in their tent, on 26 March Scott's and Lindsay's observations concurred: they were on the latitude of the station and within less than a mile of it. That same day Gino took off to look for them in the only operational Moth, carrying supplies from the base. It was the first occasion weather permitted flying since the plane's ski undercarriage had been repaired. For two hours he flew north-west seeing nothing below but a limitless extent of snow, its glittering expanse fragmented into a patchwork of black shadows by the beams of the low sun. Then Cozens, who was piloting the aircraft heard Gino's voice coming through his earphones: 'I want you to realise that you're in complete charge and can turn back as soon as you think fit.' He shouted back to say there was no need to, they still had plenty of fuel. 'Alright,' said

Gino's unhurried voice, 'But I thought I should tell you that I can see through the camera trap that the bottom of the airplane is being covered in oil.'

They made it back, to land safely on the base fjord. The problem was soon fixed – the crank-case breather had been blocked with ice – and they kept the plane lashed down on the frozen fjord so they could take off at once if the weather improved. On 1 April it made fools of them. A blizzard blew in with such force the men could not reach the airplane, even crawling on hands and knees. Three days later they found it cast up on the shore, wrecked and upside down. Hampton was still working on the other machine at Angmassalik. Again there was no plane available to support the relief party on the ice cap.

Meanwhile, Scott and the two with him had marked off a grid sixteen by three miles around the spot where they calculated Courtauld to be and started to sledge the area in a series of parallel lines. Visibility was usually no more than a few yards. A fine steady snow was falling, blotting out the contours, the terrain was lost in mist. When the low sun did appear the snowscape became a zebra pattern of bright crests and dark shadowed troughs. It was like looking for a man overboard in a rough sea.

Storms continued remorselessly, they could move only one day in three. Low on food and fuel, they used the Primus only to heat their meagre supper, not to warm the tent. They wanted to save paraffin to supply the station when they found it. Day after day they trudged behind their sledges in opaque twilight which occasionally split to segmented brilliance in the brief dazzle of the low sun. Night after night they huddled in their unheated tent, dispirited and hungry. It was a miserable, despairing time. 'Suffering that ruthless cold by day and listening to those truculent winds at night, we realised the strain which for months had been imposed on Courtauld's peace of mind,' Scott writes. 'My own small tranquillity was further shaken by each new day of unsuccessful search… We endured physically. We were young. But the mental strain remains – something you do not usually associate with the Arctic. It followed me into my dreams in the ice-rimmed tent – a man drowning nearby.'

Scott's party spent three weeks quartering the area… and could not find Courtauld. On Easter Sunday, 5 April they killed and ate a dog. They were as short of food as that. In his diary Scott calculates they could spend three more days looking for Courtauld before beginning systematically to kill the lot. They continued the search, living on their dogs. By 15 April they had remaining rations for only four days more. Obviously they had missed the station, but when and how they were uncertain. Therefore they must either cover the area again, continuing the search at the expense of a dog a day with a certainty of disaster if they failed; or else they must head back at once for base to give Gino a chance to bring in a fully-equipped search team with fresh dogs and supplies.

The decision what to do and whether or not to abandon the search is Scott's as leader of the party. It is an agonising dilemma and the choice he makes at this moment will haunt him for the rest of his life, ruining his confidence by this proof of inadequacy to the world. He is weighed down beneath an overwhelming sense of defeat as they race back to base, travelling in any weather and running the crevasses blind in darkness in dulled indifference to the risks. After six days men and dogs slide down Buggery Bank in darkness. The thick pall of clouds which hides the sky seems to have shut out the fresh air as well. After the dreadful cold of the ice plateau this night of thaw is hot and enervating. Coming off the glacier they find the snow mushy and heavy underfoot. The sledge loads are pathetically light but the exhausted half-starved dogs cannot haul them under these conditions, so they let them loose, dump the sledges and start in single file to trudge the remaining miles to base. Wet, bedraggled, they are limping home in the knowledge they have failed, so weary they can find no words to speak. Lindsay and Riley go in front to make the trail. 'I was utterly done,' Scott writes:

> There was none of the old anticipation of pleasure in return...
> I was plodding through heavy snow towards a place of inquisition. Gino had trusted me to bring back Courtauld; he would ask me why we had returned without him, and I could think of nothing but the unalterable fact... I tried to recall the arguments which had led to my decision. I could not remember them clearly, but I became doubtful of their soundness; then certain I had done the wrong thing. We should have searched till the last dog was dead and we ourselves were in danger. A life for a life, and I had shirked the issue, had come back with nothing but excuses... I had probably condemned one man to death and ruined the reputation of another.

Scott is exhausted physically and mentally. On reaching the tide crack a hundred yards from base a wave of dizziness sweeps over him, he feels so drained by despair that he sits down on an empty barrel among the discarded litter surrounding the camp and asks Riley for a cigarette. He fumbles off his gloves to light it with trembling fingers. Somehow he must summon energy and wits before bursting into the sleeping hut and facing a barrage of the inevitable questions: 'Memory of that abysmal state of mind and body is painful even after fifty years,' he writes.

His respite is not for long. The clamour of the returning dogs wakes Chapman and brings him outside to see figures emerging from the gloom. 'Who's there?' he calls, then 'Have you got Courtauld?'

'No, blast you!' Scott yells back, furious and defensive. There is a long silent pause. 'I'll go tell Gino,' says Chapman.

The Prisoner

Courtauld had first seen the weather station that would become his long home when he had arrived with Chapman's party to relieve it on 3 December. Following their arrival a blizzard raged for three days, making travel impossible. As we know, throughout that time the five men lay in the cramped nine-foot tent discussing what should be done. Courtauld had already volunteered to stay here alone, but all except Chapman were opposed to this. Wager because the plan had been for him to partner Courtauld and he thought it discredited him. D'Aeth and Bingham because they had been manning the station for the last eight weeks and knew all too well what it was like – even as a couple. Both were in poor shape. Their muscles were wasted by inactivity and they had lost weight; their sleep patterns were shot, they had experienced anxiety, terror and delusions. The *idea* of isolation had appeared peaceful, the reality was anything but. To inhabit the station while 130mph gales roared across the ice cap and blizzards battered the tent for days on end had been like living through an unremitting artillery bombardment. Bingham, the expedition doctor, had suffered such fits of anxiety he had found it hard to breathe; he had lain there unable either to relax or sleep, sweating and gasping for air.

Yet Courtauld had held firm. He reiterated his ostensible reasons for remaining, quietly but insistently. To record weather conditions here throughout the winter was essential before an air route could operate across the ice cap. To abandon the station meant failure of the expedition. He was accustomed to being alone; he was suffering from frostbite in both feet and it was painful to walk; he would like to remain.

Though the others still opposed his stay, Chapman as leader finally agreed it – with the private doubts confided to his diary that we have already seen. On 6 December Courtauld got up at 4.30 a.m. to cook breakfast for everyone. Then the others harnessed up their three dog teams and started back for base. Standing in the snow outside the tent Courtauld watched the line of men and sledges move away across the ice field in the shadowless pre-dawn light, though not for long because it was so very cold. He went back inside the tent but an hour later crawled out for a last glimpse of them. Dawn was breaking and the ice field was washed by an opalescent sheen of pink. He could just see them in the distance, a group of tiny dots headed away over the frozen desert... and then they were gone and there was nothing anywhere. Except the ice.

The tent which formed the living accommodation of the weather station had been designed by Gino in the shape of a double-skinned umbrella six feet high at the centre, fixed on curved ribs planted in the snow. The tunnel composing its entrance was dug beneath floor level so any warmth inside would not escape, but it also prevented fresh air from entering. The only ventilation was provided by a brass vent one inch in width protruding from the apex. That little metal snout would be of crucial significance in the months to come.

Riley and Lindsay, the first occupants, had made improvements to their home. The weather was relatively warm at the beginning of their shift but by mid-September they were recording external temperatures of -4°C. It was 'damnably cold' in the night; the chill woke them at 4 a.m. when they had to light the Primus to warm up. Calculating that the tent was always about 5° warmer than the air outside, they set about insulating it. Gino's textbook on cold weather survival – the only one available – was *The Friendly Arctic* by Vilhjalmar Stefansson. From it he and the rest of the party had learned (in theory at least) the technique of building snow houses. It had taken early explorers even longer to appreciate the virtue of igloos than it had to realise the value of dogs to pull sledges. By the same logic which tells us that only birds can build birds' nests, they were convinced the skill was a racial gift peculiar to the natives; white men were incapable of constructing igloos. Ernest Shackleton was aware of their advantages but himself always used tents, explaining that he had no Eskimos to erect them. Yet the snow house is the perfect natural-built dwelling in extreme weather conditions. If sufficient fuel is available it is possible to raise the temperature within to 26°C. The inner surface of the snow dome thaws but does not drip as the snow soaks up the water soon as it forms.

Cutting large blocks of snow with a long knife, the first occupants of the weather station built these up in tiers around the tent to cover it completely – except for that all-important stub of ventilating tube which poked out the top. They had learnt how to build an igloo from Stephansson but also from Flaherty's seminal film *Nanook of the North*, shot in the Canadian Arctic and released in 1922. Inside the tent-cum-igloo they constructed a sleeping platform from empty ration boxes, which they covered with reindeer skin like the floor. It was upon this that Courtauld set out his sleeping bag for his first night of single occupancy in his new residence. He did not know how long he would be living here. It might prove feasible to relieve him by airplane, if a gap in the weather coincided with suitable snow surface for landing on the ice cap. And even if that were not possible a plane could probably fly in on a clear day to resupply him by dropping food and fuel. The total provisions at the weather station at the start of his vigil consisted of:

6 ration boxes
26 gallons paraffin
2 bottles concentrated lemon juice
1 bottle cod liver oil

Each ration box was designed to last one man a fortnight, but the various sledging parties had established that one could be made to last as much as ten days longer. Earlier inhabitants of the station had consumed fuel for lighting and cooking at the rate of two gallons a week.

Courtauld had work to do here, recording the instruments. He had books to read and, most importantly, he had tobacco. 'There is nothing to complain of,' he wrote in his diary that first night alone, 'unless it be the curse of having to go out into the cold wind every three hours to observe the weather.' He was content, he had chosen this. Nobody before had ever spent a winter alone on the ice cap; this was his chance to do something big.

At long last Courtauld had escaped from his family, the rich, complacent, bourgeois family he had grown to loathe. Since infancy it had imprisoned and restrained him, preventing his becoming the man he knew he might be.

The Courtaulds were French Protestants who had fled to England to escape persecution in the seventeenth century, settling in Essex near to where they landed. It was August's great-great-uncle who had founded the family textile business, building and operating a small mill at Bocking. By the time of his death in 1881 he had amassed a fortune of £700,000 (about £55 million in today's money) almost entirely from the sale of black crepe. Black crepe was essential for mourning in the nineteenth century, and the Victorians mourned ostentatiously and long. Bereavement required its own wardrobe and the Courtaulds' mills supplied it. When the Queen died the fashion died with her, but by then they had invented a new product – artificial silk. Used for women's underclothes and stockings, cheaper and harder wearing than the real thing, it was immediately popular; when women began to show their legs flesh-coloured stockings became wildly fashionable. The family fortune had been founded on death, by extending the business into sex it prospered splendidly.

The Courtaulds were rich, but their wealth came from manufacturing and the nobs of the period looked down on trade. During the Belle Epoque the swells went to the Riviera, the Courtaulds went to the mill. Today, new money is soon made welcome but then it took a couple of generations to become acceptable. By the 1920s, August was on the same social level as those he knew at school and Cambridge, but his wealth set him apart. It constrained him, and his introverted nature was no help in surmounting the barrier it threw up. His father Samuel 'didn't make money – it came to him, as it were from the sky,' Courtauld wrote. 'He used to say that the thing about having money is that you don't have to think about it.' At his factory in the village only a short walk from the house, Samuel showed himself to be a kindly and philanthropic employer. He was a worthy and rather dull man who liked books but otherwise was determinedly philistine. He owned a town house in Kensington – which later became the Dutch embassy – and rented a grouse moor in Scotland but insisted, 'I'm like the cat, I prefer my own fireside.'

As a child August met his parents at lunch and sometimes for an hour after tea, but the only time he got to talk with his father was on the two-mile walk to the village church every Sunday. The reason for the family's flight to Britain was religion, and the Protestant faith remained important to them. Refugees by origin, they had become archetypically English: orthodox, respectable… and dull.

Children should be seen not heard, and neither for long. It was an axiom of the period, and standard practice for the upper class to have their children brought up by others. Courtauld was raised by a series of nannies and nursemaids, as were his younger sister and brother. Discipline was strict in the upstairs nursery. If the children misbehaved they were locked in a wardrobe or whipped with a bamboo switch, fresh-cut by the gardener for the punishment. Educated at home by a governess, at the age of nine he was dressed in a suit with shorts and a bowler hat then put on a train to Eastbourne. The headmaster of his prep school, a clergyman, beat him and the other boys on their bare bottoms with a cane and taught them Christian theology. 'You needn't worry yourselves about the Trinity,' he told them. 'It's quite simple, just the same as the cricket wicket. Off stump Jesus Christ, middle stump God-the-Father, leg stump the Holy Ghost: three in one and one in three.'

Courtauld was reticent by nature, and his upbringing taught him understatement. 'There was a bit of a flap on,' as he put it later, when he came home on holiday at the end of his first term. World War I had started. An underground shelter was dug in the park for protection against Zeppelin bombing but the raids provided such good fun no one considered going there. One Zeppelin flew so low over the gamekeeper's cottage he tried to down it with his shotgun. Another crashed nearby at Frinton; the German crew set fire to it before surrendering to the town's population, who were spectating the event from the sea wall, agog with excitement and delight but at a loss how to deal with arresting such celebrity visitors.

The war inspired Courtauld's imagination. With a boy's love of ships, he was determined to join the Navy; he set his heart on it. Aged thirteen, he went for an interview at the Admiralty accompanied by his father. Two weeks later he was seated in a class back at school when the headmaster came into the room to hand him a letter from the Admiralty. It said he had failed the interview. He could not help himself. In front of the headmaster, his form mistress and the whole class he broke down and wept.

Throughout his first week alone at the weather station Courtauld was kept busy. The boxes of stores lay piled in the snow outside and had to be manoeuvred through the tunnel entrance and stacked within the tent or the small igloo which served as storehouse. During that week he kept a careful check on how much food he ate and on the tobacco he was smoking. At its end he calculated for how long he could exist on the stores he possessed. Having done so he perversely decided to ignore the result, choosing instead to assume a relief party *must* succeed in reaching him by 15 March... and planned accordingly. 'I prefer to eat my cake rather than have it,' he wrote in his diary. '*carpe diem* was a tag which served as an excuse whenever I felt hungry.' By a curious coincidence, of which he was almost certainly unaware, *carpe diem* was also the motto inscribed on Gino Watkins' family crest.

On Courtauld's second day alone the sun did not show above the horizon. Arctic night closed in, yet when he dressed up in full kit of sweaters, anorak, waterproof trousers and boots, six times a day and crawled outside to read the instruments it was seldom dark. The wind had dropped on the date the others left for base and it was utterly still. The nights were starlit and a half moon bathed the pale vastness of the ice cap in a cold sheen. Sometimes the heavens were laced with colour by the arcs of the northern lights 'like purple smoke wreathes twisting and writhing all over the sky... The silence outside was almost terrible. Nothing to hear but one's heart beating and the blood ticking in one's veins.' Such moments alternated with 'those in which day and night were obliterated in one sweeping roar of blizzard showed me Nature in her most sublime and her most terrible moods.'

Once the storms returned he was kept occupied by having to dig his way out of the tunnel each time he needed to read the instruments. A blizzard would fill the tunnel mouth with snow in half an hour. 'The difficulty was that digging from the inside only piled up the debris further back in the tunnel, so that very soon the whole passage-way became filled, and only a small crawling space between the debris and the roof could be kept clear.' In time this would become an increasingly serious problem.

When he *had* dug his way out, the six-times-daily routine involved wading through knee-deep snow in the yard then climbing the six-foot drift burying the protective wall which earlier occupants of the station mistakenly had constructed. After which he had to find the instruments, often in bad light and driving snow. Once he got lost only yards from the tent. Disorientated in the whirl and bluster of the storm, it was only luck or instinct which guided him back to safety.

Between the blizzards the silence was absolute. It inspired a kind of awe in him. He was glad to be without a radio or gramophone. 'For the first month or so I was very averse to the least noise. The complete silence all round seemed to urge one to keep in tune with it by being silent oneself. After a time I got over this, and used to get great satisfaction from a sort of singing.'

Deliberately he kept his mind busy. He made astronomical calculations he had no need for, played chess against himself and read Jane Austen, Thackeray, Scott, Galsworthy, Pepys' diaries and Whitaker's Almanack which had been left by the previous residents. An extensive list exists of the books which the party took with them to the Arctic; titles are mentioned in most of their diaries and attest to that similarity of mindset they speak of which enabled them all to get on so well together. The list indicates they may have embraced the music of the new pop culture, but modern writing they did not. Which was odd, because all of them were readers and raised on books. They were schooled since childhood in the canon of English literature and poetry, their education in this field if not in others had been comprehensive. Books were important to them. Yet – true for almost all of them – their tastes stretched to the war poets but no further. The Bloomsbury group they thought pretentious and to be mocked. Joyce, Kafka, Gide and Proust they did not care for, and they did not respond to the poetry of T. S. Eliot and Pound. Obscurity and ambiguity were not to their liking, 'cleverness' was something they distrusted. In their literary tastes they were steadfastly old-fashioned.

Each day Courtauld kept up his own diary, much of it, perhaps all of it, addressed to his fiancée Mollie. His lonely New Year resolutions were to marry her... then find a house, buy a bigger boat and get a job. It was for Mollie that he was here. Food preoccupied him. Not so much cooking and eating it – for his meals were frugal, brief and monotonously similar – but thinking about it compulsively. He ate porridge, ship's biscuit, pemmican, while dreaming of feasts. He planned a banquet, drew up a list of thirty-six guests (all male, all bachelors) and composed the menu: oysters, soup, sole with mushrooms, *tournedos*, woodcock or grouse, chestnut and orange dessert, strawberry or raspberry ice, caviar or pancakes flambés.

Soon after Christmas he discovered that four gallons of his precious paraffin had leaked away. He decided he could no longer use the Primus to warm the tent but now only for cooking. A further supply of fuel lay buried outside but it took him several weeks of exploratory digging before eventually he found it beneath six foot of snow. His feet were still causing him pain; he had got frostbite in both on the journey to the station. He unwrapped the bandages to examine them. The nails had fallen off and his toes were disgusting to look at: 'V. nasty, soft, dead and gooey,' he noted. On 4 January a blizzard blew up which filled the tent's entrance with snow faster than he could clear it. He dug it out best he could but the back of the tunnel became so choked with debris he could only get through by sliding on his belly and by evening his exit was completely blocked. Trapped in the tent, he could no longer visit the weather instruments outside but only lie in his sleeping bag listening to the storm. He knew he could not clear the tunnel and was in trouble, but remained calm. 'My end should be peaceful enough and I have four slabs of chocolate to eat during it. Anyhow it won't be attended by the fuss and frills of pegging out at home.' He fell asleep but in the night woke up with a start on hearing someone call to him. Again his name was called and his heart leapt for he recognised the voice. It was Mollie.

Next day he used a knife to chip a hole in the roof of the igloo storehouse then tunnelled up through the snow to create a new way out. 'THANK GOD,' he wrote in his diary. He wedged an empty ration box in the hole to make a trapdoor and resumed his job recording the instruments. The tent was almost buried now and under the weight of snow its walls were starting to bulge in ominously. Extracts from his diary convey the weeks that followed:

Rather beastly weather... Signs of easterly fornicator [the explorers' name for a severe blizzard]... Still as death and dark as pitch. Barometer dropping like a stone. Suppose something really unpleasant is about to happen... Felt rather faint yesterday... Heart beating very fast... House shows signs of collapsing. Wish I could get snow dug off roof. Would have done so yesterday if I hadn't felt so bad... Can't stay out for more than a few minutes as feet freeze up. Finished

Guy Mannering. Jolly good book... Finished *Jane Eyre*... Only
ten gallons of paraffin left... Finished *Wuthering Heights*... A
foul gale is blowing at present and nearly succeeded, the night
before last, in blocking the snow house bolt-hole which is my
only exit... No sign of the aeroplane. I very much doubt if it
will come now...

And then on 19 February something terrifying happened. 'I was
reading in here as usual when I heard a rushing sound seeming
to come from behind, and increasing in a second to a roar like an
avalanche. It ended suddenly with a crash like thunder. I thought I
was going to be overwhelmed...'

Fear and Madness in

Perpetual Night

'We are afraid,' an Eskimo once said to the explorer Ramussen. He was describing not his feelings at that moment but the chronic condition of his race and their inherent state of mind in the Arctic. For the individual and the tribe, fear was ever present. And with good cause – the unremitting hostility of their surroundings made fear an understandable, indeed rational reaction.

Christianity had come to east Greenland early in the twentieth century; by the 1930s the two settlements on the coast each had a Christian missionary, often of mixed race for none of the Eskimos could speak Danish. The new religion co-existed with but had not displaced the ancestral myths and rituals the Eskimo had observed since prehistory. Not a Christian god but all-powerful invisible forces governed the world. He had every reason to believe in forces he could not see – can you see the wind or cold?

Spirits surrounded them, real to them as sea birds or their

dogs. Some guided and counselled them, helping them in danger. Others were malign, tormenting them with misfortune, suffering or death.

The Eskimo was afraid of death: not his own, but the death of a relative or adult member of the tribe. He was haunted by recall of his own evil deeds and of deceptions practised upon the family of the deceased, for which the dead man's spirit might seek revenge. The air was always thick with spirits, fiends rode the wind, and in the long dark of Arctic winter individuals were sometimes attacked by hysteria. Prisoners of the night, they went stir crazy, broke up the house, ate faeces, slashed themselves with knives, threw off all restraint with superhuman strength, foamed at the mouth and rushed naked and howling on the ice. And this madness came upon them while living in a community, supported by the comfort of the tribe. Never did they have to undergo that long dark alone.

When Courtauld had first arrived at the ice cap station with Chapman's party to relieve D'Aeth and Bingham, he had lain in this same tent, where he was today, discussing whether they would have to abandon the station. One of the reasons he gave for remaining here was that he was used to being alone. As noted earlier this was not true. Solitude had been impossible in childhood because of the constant presence of family and servants, and certainly it could not be found at Charterhouse, the public school where he was sent after failing the Admiralty interview. He did not distinguish himself there, either academically or at sport. He had developed a hatred of authority and here authority was exercised not just by masters but also by monitors, both of whom had the right to cane. Disliking team games, he avoided them when he could and excelled only in rifle shooting. Unpopular, he was caned often.

Though he found greater personal freedom on going up to Cambridge, he felt no more at home there. Shy and a loner, he struck others as aloof. He read engineering, but because of his poor record in maths was obliged to settle for an ordinary rather than an honours course. He joined no clubs and the social events of May Week were excruciating for him. During one ball he suggested to his partner they take a stroll by the river at the end of the lawn. Wearing evening clothes they walked silently side by side in the moonlight by the quiet water for a long time. 'Oh this is too awful,' his partner burst out at last in desperation. 'Can't you think of *anything* to say?' But he couldn't.

He had no interest in sex. 'I had no use for girls at this time and thought them a nuisance. Never really saw one at close quarters until I became engaged some years later.' And he had less and less interest in engineering. After spending several weeks in Rugby at a factory lathe as part of his degree course, on returning to Cambridge he switched to geography. His pleasures were rough shooting and sailing; his father had given him a 24-foot racing yacht. But he possessed neither passion nor ambition. Others graduating with him knew what they wanted to do, if not with their lives at least for now. Courtauld did not. Until, only shortly before coming down, he met the man who proved such an inspiration to Gino, Scott, Chapman and other undergraduates at that time. 'I discovered a tower in St John's College surmounted by James Wordie,' is how Courtauld records the event.

Wordie invited him to join the expedition he was taking to east Greenland that summer. Its purpose was to map a stretch of only partially explored coast and attempt to climb Petermann Peak, at that date unconquered and believed to be the highest mountain in the Arctic. The cost of the expedition was met by each of the seven undergraduate members subscribing £100, the rest paid by the university and Wordie himself. Chartering the *Heimland*, a small coal-burning Norwegian sealer, they all packed on board and headed for the north. Eleven days later they reached the coast of Greenland in thick fog, not knowing where they were. When the weather cleared they went ashore and, while the scientists among them worked, the rest practised revolver shooting with the weapons they had brought with them, standing sideways to their target right arm rigidly extended in the manner of the period.

The survey of the coast which followed taught Courtauld the practical use of instruments: plane table, theodolite, sextant, clinometers, psychrometers, hypsometers; the tools of exploration. They worked long shifts, for it was full summer and the sun never set. Courtauld was physically the weakest in the group but he was diligent and determined. In the course of a month they mapped 150 miles of coast and its offshore islands. No Eskimos lived that far north, but while surveying they found the remains of an abandoned settlement. A skeleton was brought on board the *Heimland*. Courtauld was appalled. Startled and rather embarrassed by his reaction, the others joked about such unscientific superstition but he remained dismayed by what they had done; he believed they had brought a curse on the ship and upon them all.

The attempt to climb Petermann Peak was a failure but two years later Courtauld sailed back to Greenland with Wordie in the *Heimland* for a second assault upon the mountain, described by the first explorers to discover it as 'a monstrous pyramid of ice.' By then he was seeing Mollie. She lived only a few miles from his home in Essex, and they had known each other since meeting at a fancy-dress party when he was fifteen and she twelve. She was intelligent, pretty, popular and highly social. She saw Courtauld, but a lot of other people too. Her life was a constant round of house parties and hunt balls, together with plays, concerts, cocktail and dinner parties in London. She did consent occasionally to sail with him at weekends, but didn't much care for the bathroom arrangements on a racing yacht. He had by now become a City stockbroker, hated his work and complained he didn't see enough of her. He was besotted, but she had many admirers; she didn't want to be tied down.

But she came up to Aberdeen to see him off to Greenland aboard the *Heimland*. After the ship had cast off and he had waved his last to her, he wrote a letter for the pilot to take ashore when he left the vessel. A reserved, cautious man, this time he held nothing back. He loved her, he said, and from this moment on all he attempted in his life would be done for her. 'If only I had the chance of doing something really big, I feel I could do it – for you.'

That summer he did not get the opportunity. 'Fate always dodges me and does me down,' he noted. Wordie's party again failed in their attempt to climb Petermann Peak, though they got to 9,600 feet. 'I didn't think he was going to last out... anyone with less courage and determination wouldn't have done so,' one of the others wrote of Courtauld. On the date the *Heimland* got back to England, Mollie departed for Venice to stay with her uncle, who was British consul there. Courtauld was bitterly disappointed. 'How can you be so cruel as to go that very day?' he demanded. He wrote her repeatedly over the next month, but her life was a hectic whirl and her answering letters few. His only consolation was sailing: 'The sea seems the only place whose sound and feel and sight and touch give me any kick now.' And then, at the end of that September of 1929, Gino Watkins came to stay as member of a house party at Courtauld's Essex home and spoke of his plans for an Arctic air route expedition...

Courtauld never discovered what it was that caused that terrifying avalanche roar rushing to engulf him and the thunderous crash which shook the tent on 19 February. But what can it have been but that immense 1½ mile-thick slab of ice splitting open? A trapdoor crashing wide into a monstrous sepulchre of ice.

Blizzards blew regularly from that date on; the temperature dropped to -40°C. Suffering badly from the cold, he dared use the Primus only briefly to cook. He lit the Aladdin lamp sparingly and passed half his time in total darkness. At the start of March he was down to his last four gallons of fuel. On the 7th he wrote in his diary, 'I reckon, unless something has gone wrong, the relief should arrive between the 15th and the end of the month. One can only trust in God.'

On the night of 19 March the wind shifted and a gale roared in from a new direction. A hole developed at the edge of his trapdoor exit and a fine jet of snow blew in with the force of a high-pressure hose. By morning the store house was completely filled; there was no way out. With great difficulty – for he was not a practical man – he chipped a hole in the roof of the other igloo, the latrine. His frost-bitten fingers made it hard to grip the knife, sharp splinters of ice rained down onto his face. It was awkward work and took ages to complete. Then he had to burrow upward through five feet of snow to reach the surface. When he finally broke through the light was blinding. It was a brilliant day; the sun was back and had risen three fingers above the horizon, flaring incandescent on the ice field. Eyes tight shut he groped for his dark goggles, drawing the pure icy air deep into his lungs after the foetor of the tight-closed tent. He stayed out there till the cold became unbearable, then improvised a covering hatch to his new exit, scrambled back down the tunnel into his malodorous lair, wormed into his damp sleeping bag in the dark, and went on waiting.

'Why is it that men come to these places?' Courtauld asks in his diary. 'In the old days it was thought to be lust for treasure... Then it was a craving for adventure... Is it curiosity, a yearning to look behind the veil onto the mysteries and desolation of nature in her forlorn places? Perhaps, but that is not all. Why leave all whom we love, all good friends, all creature comforts, all worldly joys? What do we gain?'

Why do men come? For him it was to make a journey into himself.

He wanted to find out where his limits lay, to go to the very edge to discover what he *was*. His declared reason for being here – to maintain the meteorological readings crucial to the expedition's purpose – was not the true motive. Concealed behind it lay a very different, spiritual intention. In electing to stay alone at the weather station he had embarked upon the classic route of purification and mortification leading to truth followed by mystics throughout history and known as The Way. The goal of the mystics' quest is a state of harmony with the cosmos or union with God. An extension of that fragmentary experience when a sublime view, music or art induce a sensation of awe as the mind is stilled, the self dissolves and seems to merge with a higher plane of consciousness. The Way is a series of spiritual exercises designed to facilitate and enlarge these brief encounters with the transcendental world by stripping away the superficial things which distract the mind. What it leads to is illumination: periodic exalted raptures which are the reward for having pierced through to another level of reality; the consciousness of the absolute, or sense of the presence of God.

Do we in fact morally bury ourselves in fleeing from the world?' Courtauld questions. 'Do we simply rot or grow rank like some plant thrown over the garden wall? Or do we rather come nearer to reality, see more clearly the great purpose behind it all, in stripping our souls of the protection of our friends and in putting from us the pleasures of the body? How little the worries of the world seem to one in such a situation as this; how grand and awful the things that are here, the things that grip the heart with fear, the forces that spin the universe through space. In leaving behind the transitory hopes and fears of pathetic humanity, does one come closer to the things that abide, the forces which endure?

On 22 March a gale blew up, piling a high drift of snow over the tent to cover it almost completely and stacking such a weight upon the ration box escape hatch frozen into the tunnel's mouth that it became immovable. He was unable to dig as he had left his spade outside the last time he had cleared the tunnel; the only tool remaining was his pocket-knife. Despite all his efforts he could not shift the ration box. The weather station was submerged and Courtauld was finally and completely sealed into the buried tent. He was trapped inside a gigantic ice-cube one and a half miles thick and almost a million miles in surface area – and there was no way out.

Despite his desperate situation he remained curiously serene. 'It was clearly futile to get anxious, when by no possible endeavour on my part could I make any difference to the course of events… God has kept me going so far, so perhaps He will see me the rest of the way.' 'The food situation was also becoming interesting about this time,' he noted in his diary. He had scaled his rations to last until the middle of March, and was now living on the bare residue that was left. Little paraffin remained. Each morning he warmed up a handful of oatmeal for breakfast. Lunch was a ship's biscuit, supper a few mouthfuls of raw pemmican and margarine. He was eating less than half the daily ration of food. His body had become thinner, the muscles in his legs were wasted from lack of exercise.

The most disagreeable aspect of his accommodation was the frozen condensed moisture which covered the whole inside of the tent and hung in long icicles from the roof, dripping on his face. Within his sleeping bag it had turned into ice which melted to tepid damp with his body warmth. He had to curl up to nurse his frost-bitten feet in his bare hands to prevent them freezing. He lit the lamp only for minutes at a time to keep up his diary and to read – books and the last letter he had received from Molly. 'It's the only thing left that gives me pleasure,' he wrote. Sometimes he reached out of his sleeping bag to grasp and hold the pipe she had given him as a parting gift, which served as his talisman and security blanket. Occasionally, very occasionally, he smoked it, luxuriating in the pleasure. He was down to his last tin of tobacco. 'I am completely buried. Paraffin has v. nearly run out and things are generally pretty dismal,' he wrote in his diary.

Occasionally he wormed along the tunnel to the snow house to chip around the sealed hatch with his pocket-knife. It was a ritual task he set himself though he knew it to be futile. The ice was as hard as concrete, he made little impression upon it. Over the past weeks the snow which had accumulated on the floor of the tunnel had become compressed by the pressure of his crawling through, making it smaller and smaller. 'Many times I got stuck for some considerable time ... but always managed to wriggle one way or another eventually.'

Unable to exit from his hole he could not maintain his readings of those weather instruments whose gauges were outside the tent. He had nothing else to do but lie there curled up against the cold and think. Fears gnawed at his mind. The ventilator pipe would become blocked with ice, the foul air in his lair would grow toxic and poison him. Under the weight of snow the tent creaked and sagged, it would give way and smother him beneath it. The level of snow outside was now almost to the apex of the tent; even if the relief party managed to get through how would they find him?

But they were looking for him. Unknown to Courtauld, Scott's party were less than a quarter-mile away at this time, and spending each day searching in the dim light and dreadful weather for the tent where he lay buried.

On Easter Sunday, while Scott and his party were boiling a dog for dinner within shouting distance (on a still day) of where he was, Courtauld wrote in his diary: 'Now been alone here four months. No sign of relief. Only about a cupful of paraffin left and one or two candles. Have to lie in darkness almost all the time. Chocolate finished and tobacco almost. What a change from last Easter...' And then the entry becomes a letter to Mollie, the woman he loves and had hoped – still hopes despite all odds against – to share his life with. 'If it were not for having you to think about as I lie in the dark and can't sleep, life would be intolerable. I wonder what you are doing. If I could be sure you were happy I wouldn't mind. But I trust in God absolutely. I am sure He doesn't mean me to die alone here.'

THE MEDIA PILE IN

O N 20 APRIL Scott and his party had limped back to base at 2 a.m., exhausted and demoralised after forty days on the ice cap, to tell Gino they had been unable to find Courtauld. All were ravaged by what they had gone through and suffering from frostbite, with blackened strips of skin peeling from raw faces abraded by the wind. Scott was wasted by his sense of failure, physically sickened by what he had to impart. Yet Gino took the news calmly; there was no drama. In his quiet voice he asked about weather conditions and the plan they had followed. He reassured Scott he had done the right thing. Courtauld must still have reserves of food and would be all right if he could be reached quickly.

They fed the starving dogs and went inside. Everyone was up and busy, preparing food and drink for them. All were welcoming and solicitous, hiding their anxiety. While Scott was eating Gino questioned him on what, from his experience, he considered the best plan to follow now and the best composition and equipment for the relief party. 'In a moment I had changed from an utter failure to Gino's chief adviser... He was a great leader,' says Scott.

Then Gino sat down to work out the sledge loads for his journey, his fingers playing scales on the table as always when he did sums. Stephenson, the chief surveyor, went through the mathematics of Scott's calculations. Chapman and Rymill, who would accompany Gino, assembled their kit. When later Gino did likewise he was seen to pack a prayer book. 'If he should fail to find Courtauld, or if he should find him dead, I believed it would break Gino completely as an explorer,' Scott wrote. 'But he had no room for such thoughts. He was ruthlessly calm and business-like... When he had finished... he gave his instructions, went to bed and fell asleep at once. The confidence which had been given back to me made me convinced of the reality of the hardships and difficulties which had beaten us. Most of them would remain for Gino... but at least he would not come back with excuses. Where a life was concerned he would stake everything.'

At dawn on 21 April the relief party got away on the 130-mile journey to the station. Scaling the glacier in bright sunshine, under a clear sky they sledged toward where Courtauld lay entombed, dead or alive, in his buried tent.

Before setting off Gino had sent a wireless message to the expedition committee in London explaining the situation and informing them that he was leaving with a fresh party to relieve the weather station. 'Had we been more mature we would have realised the inevitable result,' says Scott. Understandably the message caused great distress to Mollie and triggered high anxiety in Courtauld's family. His father and mother, who were in mid-Atlantic aboard the *Queen Mary*, received the news by relay and at once cabled Captain Rayner – secretary of the committee and also engaged to Courtauld's sister – instructing him to organise a rescue expedition immediately, regardless of cost. The message was also passed to *The Times*, which had reported on the expedition since its start. The story ran next day under the restrained headline 'Anxiety For Safety Of Mr Courtauld.'

Meanwhile Rayner had been cabling airlines in Canada and the United States trying to charter a powerful long-range aircraft fitted with skis and a pilot prepared to undertake the rescue mission. Unable to locate a suitable plane and fearful of the time that was being lost, he flew to Sweden and hired the experienced aviator Captain Ahrenberg to pilot a large Junkers monoplane, which carried a mechanic and wireless operator and was equipped with both floats and skis together with long-range fuel tanks.

It was an irresistible story for the media. 'Arctic Air Quest For An Explorer. Millionaire's Son Alone On Ice' was the headline of the *Daily Express*. The *Evening Standard* followed with 'Marooned In An Arctic Waste'; the *Sunday Despatch* featured 'Father's SOS From Liner – No Expense To Be Spared'; the *Daily Herald* described 'The eyes of a starving man, marooned alone in his tiny snow-hut on the lofty ice cap of Greenland... gladdened by the sight of an aeroplane swooping from the east.'

When the *Queen Mary* arrived in Southampton the press was there to interview Courtauld's parents as they disembarked. 'Mother Says, I Have No Fear', announced the *Evening Standard*. The *Daily Express* had by now tracked down Mollie: 'Meanwhile there is a girl waiting in an Essex village'. 'The Woman Who Waits' was the heading to the *Daily Telegraph* story. The *Evening Standard* raised the heat by revealing 'a further disastrous development': Gino's relief party was now also missing, and invented a despairing last wireless message from Courtauld (who of course had no radio): 'Absolutely without food'. It was all desperately upsetting for Mollie. She still had her fiancé's letter in which he spoke of doing something big – for her. Was she the cause of this? she wondered. It was an agonising thought. Friends rallied round, wrote and telephoned, but their reassurance rang false. Even Arctic experts like J. M. Wordie thought there was now no hope of finding Courtauld alive.

The news story and rescue attempts had generated their own momentum – and incongruity. A French newspaper picking up the tale assumed from Courtauld's Christian name he was a woman and reported that Mlle Augustine Courtauld, the only female member of the expedition, was trapped alone and starving in an ice cavern with thirteen males feverishly searching for her. A further absurdity occurred when an Air Force pilot engaged by Courtauld's father, who had bought him a plane, dashed off in his car at the very start of his attempt – and was arrested for speeding. In court next day he explained to the magistrate that he was on his way to the Arctic to rescue Mr Courtauld and received a mitigated fine of £1, and the Bench's good wishes.

The speedy motorist reached the far north too late to be of any help, but to the great delight of the media others were now piling in to join the rescue. The Danish government already had a ship positioned off Iceland to provide a radio beacon and communication link for Captain Ahrenberg in his Junkers monoplane, and they now sent another to the edge of Greenland's pack ice with a Professor Johannesson and sea-plane on board. Lemon, wireless operator at the base, was puzzled to receive a signal from the Professor asking the question, 'What is Courtauld looking for?' While discussing with the others how to reply to this, an answer became redundant when a further signal arrived to say the Professor had taken off but crashed after a flight lasting four minutes.

The Expedition's own Gypsy Moth – with new tailplane made from a tree root and piece of shirt cloth – was also operating from the base at this time, so there were now two ships and four airplanes engaged in the relief operation. All proved entirely useless.

On 21 April, the date Gino started from base with a relief party, Courtauld had been trapped in his hole unable to get out for almost five weeks. During that time his lair had contracted, the walls of the tent bulged in beneath the mass of snow weighing upon them. The roof was thick with icicles, and coated with soot from the oil lamp dripping in a steady drizzle of black grime.

He had only half a cup of paraffin remaining and he was already using his last candle. The chocolate was finished; on 13 April he had smoked his last pipeful of tobacco. 'There is now precious little to live for,' he noted in his diary. Yet he was sustained by 'a curious growing feeling of security.' He was convinced 'that while powerless to help myself, some outer force was in action on my side and I wasn't fated to leave my bones on the Greenland ice cap... As time went on I began to feel complete confidence. I knew that, even if Gino was having to wait for better weather, he would not let me down. I began to realise I would not be left to die. I came to know that I was held by the Everlasting Arms.'

Once they had climbed the glacier and were on the ice cap Gino and his party with their three sledges loaded with surveying instruments, a time-signal set and five weeks' food, navigated carefully as a ship steering a precise course across the ocean. For hour after hour Gino went in front, leading without looking back, the twin furrows of his ski track pointing the dogs straight toward the station. Behind him, one of the others checked his course with a compass; each other day they confirmed their position by astronomical observations. If the station was completely drifted over they were prepared to dig for it. The weather remained fine, they made good progress. On the last day of April they knew they were only a few miles from their objective. The next days were overcast; unable to take a sun-sight they could only advance by dead reckoning until they calculated they were in the area of the station. On 4 May they knew it must lie very close but a high wind was blowing; the entire landscape was submerged beneath a fluid undulating surface of moving snow.

The wind died during the night and next day dawned bright and clear. A longitude and latitude observation showed them to be about a mile north-west of the station. Strapping on their skis, Gino, Chapman and Rymill each took a dog on a leash, spread out in an extended line and started to move forward.

On the morning of 5 May, Courtauld was lying in his buried tent in darkness. His last candle had burned out five days before, the same day he had eaten the final biscuit. The only food remaining was a little pemmican and margarine and a handful of oatmeal. As he was warming a couple of spoonfuls of this in a saucepan over the Primus the jets faltered and died. He picked up the Primus and shook it. It was empty, the last of the paraffin was gone.

Advancing in a line across the snowfield in the brilliant sunlight of a cloudless spring day, almost at the same instant Gino and the two others spotted a dark speck half a mile away. A heart-stopping moment, but their elation segued into dread as they converged toward it, racing on their skis. As they drew near the dark speck became the shredded remains of a very tattered Union Jack, three-quarters hidden in the snow, but it fluttered over a scene of almost unimaginable desolation. The weather station was gone. It had been wiped out, surfaced over, covered by a snowscape flat as a calm sea with only the tops of two weather instruments, the tip of the ventilator, the ripped flag and the handle of a shovel protruding above the snow level. The view could not have been more dead. And, as Scott observed later, it is generally the gravedigger, if anyone, who leaves a spade about.

'Then,' Gino said, 'for the first time I felt really worried.' Skiing over to the inch or two of ventilating pipe showing above the surface he knelt and shouted down it...

Within the tent: 'The Primus gave its last gasp as I was melting water for the morning meal,' Courtauld recalls. 'I was lying in my bag after this so-called meal... when suddenly there was an appalling noise like a bus going by, followed by a confused yelling. I nearly jumped out of my skin. Was the house falling down at last? A second later I realised the truth. It was somebody, some real human voice, calling down the ventilator. It was a very wonderful moment. I couldn't think what to do or say...'

Then the three men crouched in the snow above the ventilator heard a feeble voice come back. 'Are you alright?' Gino shouted down the pipe.

'Yes, thank God you've come, I'm perfectly fit,' the prisoner called back. The voice was weak and tremulous from disuse yet it was the voice of a normal man. Courtauld was alive – and sane.

Next day they started back. The weather was perfect, the high air clear and pure with the sun blazing on the ice field from an azure sky. The dogs, rested and fed, pulled at a trot, knowing they were headed home. The sledge runners hissed over crisp firm snow. Crystals kicked up by the leading team floated in the atmosphere to form a glittering trail of light on which the others followed.

The winter journey to the weather station had lasted thirty-nine days, the return took only five. Towards its end a fantastic apparition formed above the horizon toward which they travelled. A mirage which Chapman describes as resembling palaces, skyscrapers, pinnacles and domes, the vision of a celestial city built of light which appeared to be their destination.

The explorer Nansen writes that 'what drives men to the polar regions is the power of the unknown over the human spirit.' Curiously he says nothing about its converse: the triumph – or otherwise – of the human spirit over the unknown. It is that victory which Courtauld experiences now as he rides on Chapman's sledge, safe and warm on the way home. A triumph which, against his wishes, is soon to be shared with a worldwide audience who over the last weeks have been caught up in his terrifying ordeal, but which at this moment is private and deeply felt. *What* he is feeling exactly, the depth of that experience and its effect upon the man who has endured it, only faintly can be imagined by that audience, by you the reader, and by this writer who is trying inadequately to convey it. What Courtauld has gone through is so far outside our own awareness we cannot fully empathise with the man riding on the sledge. Words are inadequate, music would be a better medium to describe that epiphany and how he feels. He is coming home a quiet victor, secure and whole, returning from a journey on which, without moving from his buried tent, he has travelled very far. Into solitude, into darkness, into himself. He has endured the winds, the cold, the night. Assailed by huge elemental forces, he has confronted them as a man alone. He has faced them down and held on to come through with reason and mental integrity intact. He has gained much: certainty, peace and more, much more. His wealth counts for nothing now, he knows his riches are immense.

Thirteen years earlier Ernest Shackleton described the effect of the same experience:

We... pierced the veneer of outside things. We had 'suffered, starved and triumphed, grovelled down yet grasped at glory, grown bigger in the bigness of the whole.' We had seen God in all his splendours, heard the text that nature renders. We had reached the naked soul of man.

TELL GOD TO STOP THE WHALES COMING

ON A SUNDAY

Gino's inspiration to go to the Arctic had been ignited by Raymond Priestley's lectures at university. He had been encouraged and aided in his ambition by Professor Debenham and J. M. Wordie; all three of them veteran explorers and Cambridge dons. He had also studied the subject academically, ploughing his way through the whole canon of Arctic literature since the *Journals* of Captain Cook. But the man who influenced him most in the way he had *planned* the Air-Route Expedition was Vilhjalmar Stefansson with his thesis that the Arctic was not an inimical hostile place, but friendly.

Stefansson maintained that an individual could live there without any commodity from the civilised world – except possibly a box of matches. The Eskimos did so; a white man also could be wholly self-reliant if he chose. The theory, announced in 1905 by a young ethnologist recently graduated from the University of Iowa, excited not a ripple of interest anywhere. Those who did listen briefly considered him nuts. So he proved it.

In 1907, when Stefansson went off to spend *five years* living in the Arctic (much of the time alone), the whaling industry, which until then had proved so lucrative, had gone into sharp decline. A substitute for whalebone, used throughout America and Europe in the manufacture of corsets, had been invented. Since 1889, fifteen to twenty ships had regularly passed the winter at Herschel Island in the Canadian Arctic, and during the intervening years the local Eskimo tribes had grown accustomed to 'paleface' food and manufactured articles previously unknown to them. Initially they had refused even to taste such things, but by 1907 they had come to appreciate flour, molasses, sugar, coffee and tobacco, which at first had been luxuries but now had come to be regarded as necessities.

In 1907/08 only one ship, the *Karluk*, remained throughout the winter at Herschel island and, though the vessel carried sufficient food for its crew, there was no surplus available to trade with the Eskimos. The tribes had lived for centuries on the seals, fish and game available in the area and these were still abundant, but now had become so dependent on 'civilised' food that they were convinced they were facing starvation. 'For myself I did not worry,' says Stefansson, who had recently arrived there, 'except for one thing, I had no matches.' He approached the captain of the *Karluk* and was offered a package containing one thousand. 'It seemed to me we could go a long way on that,' but the gift was quickly vetoed by the American academic with him and their party of nine Eskimos, who were all dedicated pipe smokers. So Stefansson went to the Canadian Mounted Police post at Fort Macpherson, asking to buy some matches. The commander, Sergeant Fitzgerald refused. He was friendly and remarkably open-handed in other ways, suggesting they spend the winter in a house that formed part of the barracks, and offered to provide them with food, fuel and anything else they needed – except matches. If they had matches they would set out to follow Stefansson's insane plan to travel east along the uninhabited coast, where they would certainly die. As an officer of the government he could not permit that. He explained that under the laws of the Yukon he could expel them from the country, for they had no visible means of support, but it would be easier to save their lives by refusing them matches. So instead of proceeding east as he had intended, Stefansson and his group walked off in the other direction toward the whaling station at Point Barrow, the nearest place they could buy them, a distance of 400 miles. 'We knew it would take all summer to get there...'

The story has an ironic and tragic coda, for the following year Sergeant Fitzgerald and three policemen under his command died of starvation on the comparatively simple journey from Fort Macpherson south to Dawson with the winter mail. Relying entirely on the supplies they carried with them, rather than from hunting, they were held up by prolonged storms. When food ran out they first ate their huskies, then their own leather clothing, then the harness of the dogs, and lastly their boots, before finally expiring from cold and hunger.

Stephansson remained many years in the Arctic, returning to the US only to organise further lengthy travels in the far north, each time accompanied only by two or three Eskimos and living off the land and sea for food throughout months and years on end. He was the most self-sufficient and understated individual imaginable, and his exploits were extraordinary. In his books he relates them with a gripping dullness which is hypnotic.

Gino had corresponded at length with Stephansson, who had come to London to see the expedition off in the *Quest* at its start. One of the subjects they had discussed was kayaks, and during the winter of 1930/31, Gino and some of the others had these built for them by the Eskimos at Angmagssalik. He wanted to learn to use the craft as they did to hunt seal, so that he and those with him could live off the sea in the course of the 600-mile journey by outboard motor-boat which he planned to make around the southern tip of Greenland to Julianehaab on the country's other coast.

Soon after Courtauld's return to base, Gino, Chapman and Rymill pitched their tents at Angmagssalik in order to acquire these skills from the Eskimos before they dispersed along the coast with the start of summer. The settlement consisted of a half-dozen wood-frame buildings grouped around two tall aerial masts on the bleak strip of rocky land between the inlet and the mountains. Around this meagre centre lay a suburb of irregular snow-covered hummocks: the Eskimo winter houses, each accommodating forty or so people together with their children and dogs. It was a true outpost of civilisation, and it had been set up in a community whose way of life had been the same – and self-sufficient – for thousands of years. Until now. Unlike the Canadian Arctic and west Greenland, the country's east coast had been only rarely visited by whaling ships; the period when Gino and his group were here was the last phase of innocence. Consumerism and Christianity were both only recently established. It would take no more than three further decades for the two wholly to destroy Eskimo culture, but at this moment civilisation was at a very early stage. Yet the symptoms and even some of the irreversible effects of the virus – if so it may be called – were already evident.

Pre-civilisation, the Eskimo tribe was the ideally functioning, entirely self-sufficient communist society. Existing through necessity – for in such adverse conditions it was the only system that could work – nevertheless the reason it did so smoothly perhaps lay in the fact that each community numbered no more than forty to sixty. There was no leader, they thought and acted as a group. They enjoyed complete equality, there was no conception of service or working for another person. Money did not exist.

Then the white man stepped ashore into this chilly Eden. It took the Eskimos in north Canada twenty-five years to get used to the newcomer's food, which at first they found inedible. The order in which they adopted western goods is interesting: tobacco, sugar, tea, coffee, flour, baking powder, chewing gum, clothing, jewellery, perfume, gramophones. 'It is not really that they consider bread as such excellent food,' says Stefansson, 'But rather that they know it is expensive and they... want to have their neighbours know they can afford to eat this even if it does cost money... They judge things chiefly by price, and desire them in proportion to their current market value.' While this shift toward western values was taking place money had come to be adopted as a convenient medium of exchange. The Eskimos sold furs at the nearest trading post for cash, all of which they spent immediately on rifles, food and western commodities from the same store, the only retail outlet for hundreds of miles. But, although they readily embraced the use of money, Eskimos never really managed to grasp the idea of service, of working *for* someone else. Mostly they proved unreliable and, once hired, not one understood the logic of not being paid if instead of working he did nothing.

When Gino and his party were in east Greenland at the start of the thirties the Danish government was conscientiously doing its best to protect the two Eskimo settlements on that coast from harmful outside influence. These were then still in a state almost of purity, for the pack ice discouraged ships from calling and, because the inhabitants were so few, there was little potential for trade so no reason to go there. However, by 1931 the Anmagssalik Eskimos had been permitted a controlled range of western commodities. Rifles, hunting gear, rope, knives, cloth, tobacco, chocolate, canned fruit, coffee and sugar could be obtained at the store. But that was pretty much the scope of what was available. Everything that came in from the outside world did so only once a year on the *Gertrud Rask*, and the magistrate decided what that 'everything' would consist of. No alcohol was allowed: its effect was thought with some reason to be ruinous and the law was rigidly enforced. The magistrate could also, as we know, block the introduction of sexually transmitted diseases by examining the genitals of every man who landed there.

This magistrate, a benign Dane, had no rubber gloves but possessed the absolute power of a despot in deciding which elements of civilisation the Eskimos were allowed, and which they were not. One might think that his hand controlled the spigot through which civilisation passed. Yet what he could not do was prevent the arrival of *image*. And with image the perception of status. The effects of this intangible import had been observed by Stephansson in the Canadian Arctic a quarter century before. There, following the arrival of the white storekeeper, magistrate, policeman and missionary, it was soon noticed by the Eskimos that the white man did not live in an igloo but a house. His dwelling was built of wood and had a roof of corrugated tin. The Eskimos acquired a fancy for the same. The skin tents they inhabited in summer and their stone-built communal winter huts roofed with skins were easy to keep warm; a few seal-oil lamps maintained them at a constant temperature of 15°–20°C. A wooden house required a cast iron stove fuelled by wood. The seashore of the Canadian Arctic was littered with driftwood, the accumulation of centuries, but now this was quickly used up constructing the crude sheds the Eskimo erected in clumsy imitation. It required a lot of fuel to keep these flimsy shacks warm, and with the rapid disappearance of driftwood it grew necessary to stop up ventilation, so they became almost totally sealed against fresh air. Inevitably there was a problem with sanitation in these fashionable new-style dwellings. Within a short space of time they were sinks of infection, where tuberculosis and other diseases could quickly spread.

Infection of all kinds was transmitted swiftly through family and tribe. Ironically, the white man's emphasis on cleanliness was partly to blame. Stephansson observed the consequences when he went to stay with some Eskimo acquaintances, Obayuak and his family, whom he had known five years previously. On the first night of his visit, before going to bed, his host took a bath. Obayuak had been in rude health when Stefansson had last seen him, but now his body was covered with running sores, which Stefansson was certain were syphilitic in origin. After washing thoroughly, he dried himself with a towel, rubbing it into these open lesions. His wife then washed, followed by the children. All dried themselves with the same towel. Next morning several visitors arrived for breakfast. All washed their hands and faces in the soapy water in the one bowl and used the same grimy towel. Stefansson says he expostulated to Obayuak, explaining the dangers of this practice and saying: 'Now you must not do these things any more. You must promise me that you won't take any more baths unless you each wipe with your own towel.' But they answered regretfully that they could not follow his advice because they had so few towels. God had commanded them that they must wash all over their bodies every Saturday night and must wash their hands and faces before every meal and on waking up in the morning. Their first duty was to obey God lest they fail to attain salvation, for they considered that the health of the body was of little importance compared to the welfare of the soul.

Very soon after the first trading post and store were set up in the Arctic came the missionary. He, just as much as the import of consumer goods, effected a disastrous change to the equilibrium between the Eskimo and his environment. Christianity spread very quickly through Alaska and the Canadian Arctic. Between 1905 and 1912 almost the entire coast was converted – though 'converted' is not the correct word, for Eskimos accepted the new faith while still retaining their own religion. This consisted of a belief in spirits together with the keeping of taboos, an extensive series of no-nos to which were now added the whole range of Christian prohibitions. All this the Eskimos observed strictly, for they had developed a lively fear of hell and eternal punishment.

Along with the ruinous precept that cleanliness is next to godliness, the missionary had taught the commandment 'Thou shalt not work on the Sabbath day.' Observing this divine injunction disrupted the work pattern of centuries. At Point Barrow in Alaska the whaling season, which lasted only six weeks, started when the ice began to break up in summer and a passage opened for whales to migrate from the Pacific to the Beaufort Sea. The Eskimos had been accustomed to camp here on the ice with boats and hunting gear to await them. Their arrival was erratic, sometimes a week or more would pass without a sighting, sometimes hundreds went by on a single day. Occasionally this was a Sunday.

When the Eskimos learned that God forbade work on the Sabbath they pulled back their boats from the edge of the ice on Saturday afternoon, secured them, and safely stashed their hunting gear before sledging back to the settlement for Sunday church services. Returning to the hunting grounds and getting everything ready again took all of Monday, so they lost two and a half days out of every seven during the short season.

Dr Marsh, their missionary in 1910, was an enlightened man. He explained to his flock that not only were they missing out on whales but they risked losing their boats and hunting gear if a gale blew up at the weekend. In response they told him to ask God to stop the whales coming on a Sunday, and not to make gales at the weekend. Their pastor's reluctance to pass on this request was unacceptable to his parishioners; *other* missionaries taught that God would grant anything they prayed for in his name. *That* was the sort of missionary they required. So they formulated charges: that Dr Marsh encouraged Sabbath law breaking, that he taught that prayers were of no avail, that he encouraged immodesty by

Spring 1931. Courtauld had been marooned alone on the ice cap all winter. Scott's party had failed to find him and turned back, eating their dogs to survive. Then the only Moth still airworthy was wrecked; there was no plane to search for him.

A desperate attempt. On 21 April Gino set out to rescue him, after Scott's party had turned back.

The women who waited. Pam Watkins (left), Gino's sister and later Scott's wife, and Courtauld's fiancée Molly (below).

Competely buried.
The ice cap station when Gino's party discovered it in May 1931.

'Are you alright?' *Gino speaking to Courtauld through the ventilator.*

Digging him out. *The top of the ventilator is visible on the left.*

'I'm perfectly fit.' *Courtauld emerging after five months alone at the ice-cap station, for the last six weeks entombed beneath the ice without heat or light, short of food and unable to dispose of his own body waste.*

Courtauld back at base camp. *The winter journey to the weather station has lasted thirty-nine days, the return took only five.*

Base camp. *Gino (centre) at the start of the southern voyage. Courtauld wanted only to get back and marry Molly, and Gino's plan to chart the coastal mountains by a journey of 600 miles in an 18 foot boat while living only by hunting, struck him as 'suicidal folly'.*

Yet he went. *Gino and Captain Lemon were in no hurry They were content to remain indefinitely in the Eskimos' 'domesticity of blood and blubber'.*

Spring 1932. *About to return to the Arctic to complete the survey, Gino asked Margot Graham to marry him. The proposal was oddly timed for a man planning not to see his fiancée again for a year.*

Back in Greenland. *The party brought no food but relied on Gino's hunting. He knew how to roll the kayak and right it if it capsized – he had total mastery of the craft. Nevertheless he took risks; the best hunting was to be found close to the edge of the glacier...*

Summer 1932. *Charles Lindbergh and his wife land at Anmagssalik after crossing the ice cap in five hours, enjoying an in-flight picnic on the way. Anne Lindbergh was first passenger to fly an air route still in use today.*

taking off his coat in Eskimo homes. These were written down by an Eskimo who had been away to school, and sent to the Presbyterian Board of Home Missions in New York. Dr Marsh was dismissed from his post in the summer of 1912.

Gino stayed with the Eskimos at Angmagssalik until the beginning of July. The settlement became the expedition's training camp when he was joined by other members of the company for two or three weeks at a time. Eleven of the party had kayaks built for them. All learnt the management of them and some to hunt, though none became so skilled in both as Gino himself.

Spring had come to the coast. The sun was back, saxifrages and harebells flowered around the settlement and green moss showed between the rocks where the snow had melted. The upside-down reflection of snow-capped mountains and blue sky trembled on the placid water of the fjord and Arctic terns wheeled and screamed in the air above as the explorers carried their kayaks down to the shore to join the Eskimo fleet at the start of the day's hunt.

There had been no question of buying already-built kayaks. Each had been constructed to fit its owner precisely as a pair of custom-built shoes. The Europeans were taller and heavier than Eskimos and their craft significantly larger. Not longer but deeper, with buoyancy matched to its owner's weight and deck just covering his thighs and outstretched legs. The framework was of lengths of driftwood spliced together over lateral ribs – carved with a penknife then steamed over a cooking pot and bent into shape – to form a skeleton eighteen feet long and two wide. The skins of a couple of bladder-nosed seals were used to cover each craft. These had been allowed to putrefy so hair and grain could be easily scraped off and the smell was nauseating. Chapman was sickened to see the women who did this work gobbling up the trimmings of hair and rotten skin with gusto. The hides were soaked and sewed onto the frame while still wet; when dry they fitted taut as a drum. The function of the slats of ivory forming the boat's keel was not to steady it but only to protect the skin if the kayak had to be dragged over ice. The craft rocked crazily; it was precariously unstable and could be capsized by any false movement of its occupant.

Gino had painted his own kayak white to make it less noticeable among the ice floes. With her slim graceful lines she looked a thing of speed, a thoroughbred of her type, says Scott, 'but a dangerous toy for a man who could not handle her.' Like the Eskimos Gino wore a waterproof sealskin coat, its hood drawn tightly around the face by a thong, whose skirts fitted exactly around the cockpit rim to create a waterproof seal. Man and boat were one. If the craft capsized – and they did often while the explorers were learning – there was no chance for the occupant to free himself. He hung trapped upside down underwater until he drowned. He must learn to roll the kayak upright again by a broad sweep with his paddle. The Europeans had spent hour after hour practising the technique, each with an Eskimo nearby in his kayak so he could haul himself up by grasping its hull if he failed in the manoeuvre. It was vital a man should know how to perform it if he hunted alone, and an indication of the Eskimo's careless attitude to death that, despite the fact that kayak drownings accounted for around a quarter of the tribe's mortality rate, a significant minority of the Eskimo hunters had not bothered to acquire the skill.

Gino and the two Europeans launching their kayaks in the fjord with the Eskimos that morning all had learned how to right the craft if they capsized, but only Gino knew how to do it with his hand alone if he had lost his paddle. He could do things with his kayak few of the Eskimos could accomplish, says Scott; he could make it get up and dance.

Once the small fleet of kayaks reached the mouth of the fjord they split up into groups of two or three to hunt the leads of open water dividing the pack-ice into a slowly shifting maze. For companionship and safety the Eskimos preferred to hunt in company; Gino did not. He had studied their methods and gained much from them, but he realised that a single man has a better chance to stalk his prey undetected. In his work he avoided risks whenever possible, but now his object was to kill seals and so he went alone. 'His enthusiasm came from pleasure in his work, but his single-mindedness from the fact that he considered it as work and not as pleasure,' Scott writes. 'He was the primitive man in search of food. Yet he was a savage with a highly trained mind. His ability to start reasonably from the beginning and hold to essentials gave him an advantage over the natives...'

Hunting from a kayak and building snow igloos had been considered purely 'native' skills by early explorers. And so had the ability to find the way blind across broken country, apparently by instinct. Not so, claimed Stefansson – white men were better at it. An Eskimo could only find his way 'intuitively' in darkness and bad weather if the ground was familiar to him. In unknown country, according to Stefansson, he could retrace his own winding trail capably as an animal but he did not approach navigation with any logic.

High upon an iceberg's crag a cormorant stands motionless with wings extended like a heraldic beast, then launches forward to flap twice and glide in a long slant above the floating pack ice. The gulls with their far-off cries show up as bright flecks in the clear blue sky, and the pack is a blaze of radiance beneath a peach-silver sun.

Gino's kayak slides effortlessly down leads of blue-black water, propelled by long strokes of the double paddle. Drops of moisture flick from the blades, glinting in the light. The cold purity of the air knifes into his lungs. With the same swift balance as a racing bicycle the craft skims through a panorama of splintered light. Points of fire wink from the facets of the drifting ice as he scoots past. In among the broken pack he is surrounded by ice floes of every size, zigzagging his way through a floating white mosaic, glistening, flaring and refracting colour in the brilliance. Fluid greenish masses of submerged ice undulate beneath the water as the kayak cuts across the surface. Braking the craft with a backstroke of the paddle, Gino noses it around the edge of a small berg, scanning the view on the other side. He sees a black head moving in the water fifty yards ahead. He freezes and holds still, intent on his quarry. As the kayak's drift brings it clear of the iceberg the seal spots the unfamiliar shape and dives.

Gino flicks his craft across the still sea to where he thinks the beast will come up among the floes and waits, poised and tense. It is not all guesswork, though guessing is part of it. The animal is not a bladder-nose but a fjord seal, which means it can stay submerged only for a few minutes. The short time he has watched it has told him so, and that it is fishing not travelling. He has learned and is an experienced hunter now; it has taken him only a short while to become skilled in the technique. The instinct which lies embedded in all of us has developed naturally within him and the Cambridge undergraduate has effortlessly regressed several millennia to become the elemental hunter with his spear.

A black head the size of a rugby ball breaks the surface twenty-five yards away among the brash-ice, at right angles to the kayak. An impossible shot – the twist of Gino's torso and recoil of the rifle would capsize him. He does not turn his head, does not move a muscle, the kayak floats still and almost invisible against the shimmering incandescence of the floe's white wall. Unaware of danger, the seal resumes fishing and swims slowly out of sight behind a floe. Two deep thrusts of the paddle speed the kayal across the surface. It is so light it can move as fast as a startled fish. When he comes around the corner of the floe Gino already has the rifle in his hand. The seal's head shows twenty yards on his quarter. He sights and fires in one movement. Slipping the rifle beneath its retaining strap on deck, he grabs the paddle. Two strokes drive the kayak forward. Taking up the harpoon, he flings it at his sinking prey to secure it before it slides from sight. Pulling up to it on the cord, he attaches the animal's body to the sealskin bladder carried on the back of the kayak for this purpose, then punctures a hole in the skin with a knife. Setting his mouth to this, he inflates the carcass as one does a balloon, stopping the hole with a leather plug. Attaching a line to the now buoyant carcass, he tows it back to the encampment, the tribe's leader bringing home the kill. 'The idea that hunting was a sport governed by conventions belonged to another world,' says Scott. 'He was the primitive man in search of food.'

Living off the land, or rather the sea, was entirely feasible on a long coastal journey, Gino decided. All the explorers concurred with him but it was generally agreed that the habitual diet of boiled seal meat, although healthy and oddly enough nutritionally satisfactory, *was* a bit boring. But they had not then experienced the full range of Eskimo cuisine, its delicacies and luxuries; they hadn't tasted its gourmet delights. Just before the inhabitants of the settlement dispersed to their summer hunting grounds and their own return to base camp to prepare for the coastal journey, the Eskimos gave a feast for them. Served by the hunters' wives, whose teeth were worn down to stumps by their daily chore of chewing skins to soften them, the banquet took place in the damp fug of one of the winter houses redolent with the appetising smell of meat, fat, urine, stale sweat and tobacco.

MENU

—⟨⟩—

Amuse-bouches of seals' eyeballs in own slime.

*Walrus brains in an emulsion of narwhale fat whisked
to a greasy froth with water. Served chilled.*

*Mattak: mouthwatering strips of narwhale skin,
presented raw in bloody jus.*

*Oraneg: Matured partridge droppings mixed with
seal fat, beaten and boiled. A popular combo
with the rich aroma of hot shit.*

*Kiviak: Putrescent guillemots prepared in the
traditional fashion compressed in a rotting mass
under a pile of heavy stones until table-ripe.*

—⟨⟩—

The last item was a particular speciality. Ceremonially the dish was offered first to Gino, seated with his party among the hunters and drinking vintage ice water like the rest. From the congealed mound of corpses in the dish Gino prised off one small compressed bird. He pulled on a leg and the rotted carcass slid off its bones like a soft wet glove into his hand. Flesh, fat, heart, coagulated blood ran down his fingers. Watched with horrified fascination by the Europeans, he raised it to his lips and let the speciality melt slowly in his mouth.

Not all the explorers felt the same about that Menu Gastronomique either during the meal or after. Though no one wanted to admit to what he really thought, some of them privately felt quite green at the memory of it, but everyone did their pallid best to agree when Gino maintained that he had found it an utterly delicious dinner, one of the best he had ever tasted. But then he would.

GOING NATIVE

THE PURPOSE OF the expedition was, as we know, to pioneer an air route across Greenland. This required establishing wind and weather conditions throughout winter on the ice cap, and charting and calculating the height of the coastal mountains north and south of Angmagssalik.

The first of these objectives had been largely fulfilled by Courtauld who had kept up his readings of the meteorological instruments outside the tent until the exit had become sealed, and maintained the barograph and thermograph inside his burrow until his rescue in May. The second intention had also been completed when the *Quest* penetrated 250 miles north soon after the explorers arrival in Greenland the previous summer. But the attempt with Scott to chart the inside edge of the coastal mountains to the south had failed; they had been defeated by winter blizzards.

What Gino now planned was to rectify this omission by charting these mountains from their *seaward* side by sailing the length of the country to the southern tip of Greenland and around it to Julianehaab on the west coast. His proposal was to make this journey of 600 miles down an only part-mapped coast, uninhabited except for a few Eskimo settlements, in an open 18-foot boat powered by a three-horse-power outboard motor. When he first exposed it to the others the plan had struck Courtauld – who, unlike Gino, knew a great deal about boats – as barking mad. 'Suicidal folly,' he called it. He pointed out that the fuel for the trip, together with a crew of three, would leave no space for food. If the engine should break down or they were wrecked they would be cast ashore on a hostile coast with no chance of walking out and none of rescue. Gino's insouciant reply was that there was no need to carry food, they would take kayaks with them and live by hunting, but yes Courtauld was right: it would probably be a good idea to take a second boat along as well.

Greenland, showing the major journeys of the expedition

Despite lively reservations and his experience on the ice cap, which had made him determine never to go exploring again, a few weeks later Courtauld found himself agreeing to join the party. 'It is utterly bloody I know,' he wrote to Mollie, 'but what else can I do? Gino wants another man for his journey, so how can I get out of it on the plea that I want to go home? I feel a frightful rotter about it, but I know what you would have me do in your heart of hearts.' The third man making up the group was Captain Lemon, the radio operator who had spent most of the year at base camp, had an Eskimo girlfriend, loved what he knew of the Arctic and relished the prospect of an adventure.

In preparation for the journey they set up a fuel dump at Umivik, 150 miles to the south – though that bald statement utterly fails to convey the flavour of the attempt, whose comical absurdity can only be realised properly by the flickering images of silent movie farce accompanied by subtitles:

Nicodemudgy, an old Eskimo who has worked as a handyman at the base is persuaded to take his extensive family to winter at Umivik. He agrees readily, explaining that he requires a new umiak to make the trip. His existing boat is loaded with his large family together with a mountainous top-heavy cargo of all their possessions then towed sixty miles to where an Eskimo is said to have an umiak for sale. The part-exchange concluded, family and possessions transfer to new vessel and set off. Almost at once they meet with disaster when they hit an ice floe which rips a gash in the boat. Panic as the umiak sinks fast. Maximum confusion and drama as family rescue themselves and best part of goods onto an ice floe. Women hastily sew up slit in umiak. Boat is reloaded with possessions. Voyage recommences with all rowing hard – but umiak goes round in a circle. Nicodemudgy now realises the keel is warped, boat won't steer straight, he's bought a bummer. Return to seller, big dispute, another umiak acquired.

'Finally he got off... with his family and wife (his third), his son, his four daughters, his granddaughter, one child of eight that his son-in-law had lent him, two sledges, ten dogs, his tent, and a year's supplies.' Plus Gino's twenty-seven gallons of petrol. All of this in a 28-foot sealskin boat. 'An Eskimo removal is an imposing sight,' Courtauld reports.

Three weeks later, on 15 August, Gino, Courtauld and Lemon followed them in two whaleboats carrying three kayaks, guns, rifles, revolvers, three sledges with man-harness to haul these over the ice cap if they were shipwrecked, a bulky wireless transmitter/receiver, a box of survey instruments, some tea, sugar, oatmeal and suet but no other food. The suet had arrived in the *Gustav Holm*, the Danish supply ship which had just paid its annual visit to Anmagssalik (and left taking six members of the expedition back to Europe). It was something Courtauld had been craving for a year. He had first requested suet the previous summer when the *Quest* had sailed to pick up the forgotten ski-undercarriages for the aircraft, but his morse message was wrongly transcribed and instead he had received a suit.

Their Eskimo friends sat on the rocks and wept when the party left, but saw them come back an hour later because Lemon had forgotten the petrol funnel necessary to fill the outboards' tanks. They set off again with one boat towing the other to save fuel. For ten days the weather held good as they motored down the coast between rocky islands and floating icebergs, landing to set up survey positions on shore. There Courtauld and Lemon made their observations and drew the map while Gino went hunting in his kayak. Courtauld writes:

The country is very lovely just now. One walks in valleys deep with moss and grasses, with thick patches of harebells in full bloom and saxifrages of many sorts. All round are the soaring peaks standing clear against the blue unclouded sky, while between them wind the many arms of deep fjords studded with fantastically shaped icebergs. To seaward the pack ice gleams white to the horizon...

Courtauld had set aside his well-founded anxieties about the journey they had embarked upon. This was a good time for him, and when they finally reached Julianehaab he would be going home – or rather back to England to marry Mollie, for home in the shape of his family had no appeal for him whatever. He was furious at their involvement in his 'rescue', at all the fuss and drama and media attention. A modest retiring man, he had an abhorrence of publicity and was disgusted by the circus he had occasioned. 'Take no notice hysterical rescue nonsense,' he had cabled Mollie when he got back from the ice cap. 'Relief carried out as part of ordinary programme. No danger. Love.' In a letter to her soon after he wrote, 'This press rot is all completely obscene... I have been so very rude to everybody about this absurd relief – and I gather the family have spent thousands on it and being in the wrong must make them all angrier – that I don't suppose they will speak to me again.'

Only one white man had previously traversed this coast when in the 1880s a Danish explorer had travelled up it with Eskimos in an umiak to discover the settlement of Angmagssalik. Unable to establish exact longitudes and lacking time to chart the offshore islands and many fjords, the map he made was tentative and incomplete. Gino hoped to improve it – particularly the detail and height of the coastal mountains, which an airplane would have to overfly – as far as Umivik. From there he planned to travel as fast as possible to the tip of Greenland and around it to Julianehaab, where they would wait for a ship to take them home. That at least was what Courtauld had *understood* to be Gino's intention.

On the tenth day of travel and surveying they reached Pikiutlek Island, which they called Pigsty. The mountains inland were slashed by deep fjords running between bare cliffs and the island too was of bare weathered rock. There was no vegetation at all, yet Lemon described it as 'an attractive spot'. Here they passed three days surveying the fjords before stumbling on an encampment of thirty Eskimos who at the end of summer would return to Angmagssalik to trade the skins and ivory they had acquired by hunting. Some were already known to the explorers from the previous winter and this was a reunion of old friends. The new arrivals shifted their camp to theirs and twenty Eskimos had supper with them that evening in a two-man tent. Hunting was particularly good here, the Eskimos said, and polar bears were numerous. A storm provided an excuse for remaining, but even when it blew out they stayed on. Courtauld was impatient to get going but Gino and Lemon were in no hurry to continue. 'He [Gino] said we were going to stay here two days and we have been five already. It is very pleasant but I want to get home,' Courtauld wrote.

They stayed on… and on. Their visit extended to nine days before they started again with enough meat to last them for the rest of the journey. The weather had deteriorated but, still towing one boat behind the other on a fifty-foot rope, they made it to Umivik in two days. On arriving they could see no sign of Nicodemudgy's camp. Stopping the outboard motor they drifted on the swell and Gino, who had very acute hearing, said he heard a dog bark. Four children came running across the rocks to meet them. They had been abandoned on an island with very little food while the rest of the family in their typically casual way had gone off for several days to hunt, leaving the girls to look after themselves. But they were living in the comfortable winter home Nicodemudgy had built and the explorers moved in on them with a welcome house present of raw seal meat. They were received with open arms.

To Courtauld's mounting frustration they remained for a week. 'It was the finest place for seals I'd ever seen,' said Lemon, but that was not all that attracted him to the location. His job as radio operator had largely denied him the travels of the others, but living with the three Eskimo girls at the base had brought him to enjoy the domestic rhythm of Arctic life. Another factor contributed to the satisfaction he found in it: in England he was judged an unattractive, even ugly man – here he was not. Lemon had been first of the explorers to take an Eskimo lover. The second was Chapman, who now had returned to Europe in the annual supply ship. During the three months between getting back after Courtauld's rescue and sailing for home Chapman had remained at base with Gertrud, who was now openly acknowledged as his mistress. Recognised rather than acknowledged perhaps, for the relationship that he, Lemon and Gino enjoyed with the Eskimo girls got up the noses of some of the party. One of them, Lindsay, wrote:

> Watkins' bunk was just above mine and every time this bloody
> Eskimo girl got up into his bunk she had to put her feet within
> an inch or two of my face. I objected strongly, and so did some
> of the others, and if the ship hadn't come when it did we'd
> have formed up and said look here, Gino, this has bloody-well
> got to stop.

Gertrude had been happy to see Chapman back from the ice cap, as she had thought him and the rescue party dead. She received him warmly. Sexual activity among the Eskimos peaked in summer; most births took place in early spring. Their breeding cycle accorded with nature's logic, but also the communal winter house was hardly the ideal place for lovemaking. In courtship they were inhibited and prudish, in marriage they remained so. Kissing on the mouth and genitals was taboo, even the mention of it was deeply shocking.

'I caress her belly, her loins, her breasts and her nipples,' an Eskimo explained to Jean Malaurie. As for kissing always on the nose and the tip of the nose... When we make love I always lie on top of her... Of course I never touch her vagina or anus, my wife would strike my hand away. She would think it would kill her or make her bear deformed children.' The man went on to provide a further slant on Eskimo sexuality: 'We desire each other only at certain times of the year... I never feel desire while hunting. It's really as if hunting took away all desire – which is all to the good. As you know the Inuit do not masturbate; it would weaken them completely.'

Among adolescent males the restrictions of communal living and innumerable taboos drove some of the young men to extreme measures, Malaurie reports:

> Occasionally [they] attempt sexual arousal by suspending themselves with a leather thong from the edge of a small cliff; they... squeeze their necks until they are nearly strangled. Hanging can indeed cause extraordinary genital arousal... The practice has caused a number of accidents in Thule.

Yet young women like Gertrude were allowed considerable pre-marital sexual freedom. Once a girl reached puberty she was *allernersuit*, impure, and a mass of taboos accompanied her monthly periods. She had to wear her hood at all times outside the house; she could urinate on icebergs (freshwater ice and sons of the land) but not on the pack ice (salt water and daughter of the sea), where she was not allowed even to walk. In certain cases she was forbidden to drink water that came from the land (freshwater ice) but had to make do with snow. When pregnant a woman was believed to be filled with uncontrollable forces threatening to the stability of the tribe. So far as was possible she stayed apart from others. After giving birth she cut the umbilical cord herself, cleaning the baby with her tongue before wrapping it in a hare's pelt, continuing throughout infancy to care for it and wipe its tiny soiled bottom in the same way. The child was not weaned until it was three or four, sometimes as old as eight. In hard times when hunting was bad no Eskimo couple could keep more than two children, preferably boys. A minimum number of girls – only the very strongest – were allowed to survive. Unwanted, deformed or mentally deficient infants were killed at birth; the mother strangled the child or smothered it with a handful of snow.

It was startling for Chapman, just before leaving for Europe in the *Gertrud Rask,* to learn from Gertrude that she was pregnant. We have no record of his reactions or how the parting played, but we know that as the ship sailed from Angmagssalik harbour many things were on his mind: the responsibility of dealing with the Courtauld family and expedition committee in London; the fact that Gino had authorised him to write the official book; that he had now somehow to start earning money; his prospects and his future. And we know that among those things preoccupying him was the thought that Gertrude was carrying his child.

With their arrival at Umivik the survey work of Gino's boat party was finished. From here the plan had been to motor fast for the tip of Greenland, round it to Julianehaab and home. Yet, to Courtauld's irritation, a week had gone by and still they lingered among the Eskimos. Gino and Lemon spent the days hunting with them. At night they would all eat in Nicodemudgy's winter house, listening to and telling stories. All by now had learnt a pidgin version of the language, and as every story on both sides was about hunting – for the Eskimos had not the slightest curiosity about the European's world and the only thing of any interest to them was hunting – communication was in its singular way excellent.

Courtauld was struck by the enthusiasm with which his two

companions embraced this brutish elemental lifestyle. It seemed to suit them well, far too well in Courtauld's view, and the realisation that they would be quite happy to join the Eskimos indefinitely in their 'domesticity of blood and blubber' was disgusting and alarming. His dismay was the standard reaction of a nineteenth-century Englishman stationed in the tropics to the horrified awareness that one (or in this case two) of his own kind had stepped outside the bounds which defined them as a caste – *they had gone native*. The perception separated him from them. He grew increasingly frantic with impatience at stopping there. He didn't want to object to something they seemed to enjoy so much, he had no desire to be a spoilsport, but his agenda was different from theirs. Both of them appeared blithely unconcerned that winter was approaching, days growing shorter and ice already forming in the fjords. It would be disastrous to become trapped here by the pack ice, but he suspected Gino and Lemon did not think the same.

When they did finally resume their journey they travelled only two days before the wind blew up and the weather turned bad. They carried on in driving rain down a channel of heaving water between a line of icebergs and the shore until one engine, then the other, broke down. 'I signalled the others to get the oars out and row,' says Courtauld. To do so they had to clear their foredeck of a mass of raw seal meat and put a kayak overboard, then they started to give way with the oars. Rowing hard they made it through a narrow passage between two icebergs and had the luck to find an island with a narrow creek ending in a beach where they ran the two boats ashore.

'We said thank God and made camp,' Courtauld writes in his diary. 'It was just in time, for it then came on to blow a real gale. The sea was thrown up the cliffs in high spurts and the rain came down in sheets. The noise of the sea was like continuous thunder. It pelted with rain and blew all next day... Going out in the late afternoon we found a dark greenish sky of low clouds from which the rain descended in sheets. All round the streams were raging and roaring down from the crags above the bay, while out at the mouth the sea thundered against the rocks. The boats were being banged about by the ice at high water and were half full. The wireless looks unlikely ever to work again.

On the fourth day the storm showed signs of stopping. Gino and Lemon went off together to climb the cliffs and get a view to the south, leaving Courtauld in the tent. They came back a couple of hours later in blithe spirits to report that the coast was thick with pack ice. Gino said they might have to remain here until next spring; he appeared quite happy with the idea of doing so. Courtauld was appalled. 'Gino and Lemon talk of nothing now but plans for wintering... This is bad news for me. It is the last thing I want to do, but Gino seems to want any excuse for staying and Lemon backs him up. I have said nothing yet, but my opinion is never consulted...'

That evening, to their astonishment, they heard the sound of a motorboat. 'This was as unexpected as the noise of a waterfall would be in Kensington.' Gino ran up a hill to light a petrol-soaked rag but it was not seen. Very disappointed, they decided it was probably the Danish explorer Ramussen whom they knew to be travelling in the area. Next morning the weather was perfect. The sun shone in a clear sky, the wind had dropped and the sea was calming. Courtauld and Lemon spent the entire day working on the outboard motors. They could get neither to run, but Lemon managed to fix the radio transmitter though not the receiver. They sent a last message saying they might try to cross the ice cap or spend the winter where they were – but did not give their position to ensure no one tried to rescue them. On the following day Courtauld succeeded in getting one of the outboards to function. Abandoning everything inessential including the radio and one boat, they crowded into the other.

Keeping the engine going continuously by refilling it with petrol from a teapot while moving, they resumed their voyage through thickening pack ice toward the inhabited west coast of Greenland.

Several weeks earlier two sledging parties had left base camp headed for separate destinations on the same coast. Rymill and Hampton were aiming for Holsteinsberg, where they would be able to find a ship to take them home. The other party, led by Scott, headed in a diagonal line south west across the ice cap toward Ivigtut, the settlement and trading post adjacent to Gino's own destination.

The purpose of Scott's mission was to establish the existence or not of that traverse valley bisecting the country – permitting an aircraft to overfly it at lower altitude – which he and Gino had failed to find on their previous unsuccessful journey south. With him were Lindsay, Stephenson and three teams of nine dogs. They travelled across the ice cap at night – at this season the sun was below the horizon for less than two hours – and through the morning until its warmth caused the surface to melt and become sticky.

On a clear evening it began to freeze early. Long before midnight it was covered with a thin crust of ice on which friction was reduced to a minimum. The weight of the sledge was immaterial, and on skis, grasping the handlebars with one hand and a ski-stick with the other, we glided along quite tirelessly until the sun rose high in the heavens and the snow crust sweated beneath our feet.

The weather was fine, the days so warm they slept naked on top of their down sleeping-bags. Sometimes it was too hot to sleep. Stripped bare in the tent they played games from the *Week-End Book* and read. They talked of home 'which seemed nearer than it had in many months.' On 20 July they reached 9,200 feet, their highest point on the spine of the ice cap, and started to descend on the other side. The wind was behind them. They hoisted sails on the sledges controlled by cords attached to the handlebars and ran downwind with the dogs racing ahead. The first night they sailed twenty-six miles. It was a hectic form of winter sport says Scott, the irregularity of the surface turned their skis. 'I was in terror that I should fall and lose my hold on the sledge, for... the dogs would run on to Ivigtut without me. It seemed like surf riding behind a one-man yacht in mid-Atlantic.'

The sun shone brightly on this Arctic idyll. For Lindsay and Stephenson it was the joyous high point of the year's expedition but Scott found himself unable to respond as freely as they. The journey was easy; he had wanted it to be hard. He had welcomed the chance to undertake it as he had longed to be away from the crowded base hut, where he wasn't comfortable among such high spirits. He felt awkward and diminished by his inability to find Courtauld. He was haunted by the memory of those sightless days tramping through a void of drifting snow and the nightmare that his comrade was drowning nearby. His failure had completely altered Scott's image of himself. His confidence and with it his personality had taken a mortal wound; he would never again be wholly at ease in his own skin, never certain, never sure. He remained an irreparably damaged man, whose transient remedy could be found only in drink.

On 28 July, Scott and his party arrived at the head of Ivigtut glacier which led down to the fjord and trading settlement. 'Then towards midnight came the most unpleasant job of all. In south-west Greenland there are cows and sheep. Huskies and domestic animals cannot live together and we had been told that we must kill our dogs... Afterwards I sat for a while on the moraine and made my peace before crawling into the tent, where there was no privacy. I read Lycidas and went to sleep.'

Next morning they threaded their way through a maze of glaciers to the land beside the shore. There they walked through clumps of willows and hazels, disturbing the bushes as they passed so great clouds of insects rose about them. They breathed them, sneezed them, swallowed them when they opened their mouths to swear. Suddenly around a corner they got a view of the tin roofs of the settlement, the harbour and the cargo boat which would take them home to Europe. Scott looked down and saw at his feet an empty beer bottle. They were back in the world of man.

Travelling the last 200 miles down the coast toward Cape Farewell, the tip of Greenland, Gino, Courtauld and Lemon had reached the most critical stage of their journey. It was too late to return, the way back to Angmagssalik was blocked by new ice; if cast ashore here the mountains were too steep to climb onto the ice cap pulling sledges; if marooned, the hunting too poor to sustain them through the winter. They *had* to make it to the west coast.

The next two weeks were a nightmare. Glimpses of Courtauld's diary convey the cold wet misery of their journey.

We started at 2.30 a.m. and got involved in thick brash ice. We went twelve miles out to sea to get round the brash ice, but could not see the end of it and had to put back. In the evening the rain set in. Gino woke with his body half under water and only his head above. However, he refused to take a dry change of clothes of mine, and having moved to a drier patch composed himself to sleep again. *22 September*: The fog cleared. Engine refused to work. Ice sheathing peeled off. Had to row back half-full and leaking like a sieve. After repairs moved camp to a more sheltered place. Got there with great difficulty in heavy swell.

The diary continues:

23 September: Fine day but had to beach boat to repair leak caused by the bumping on the rocks… *24 September*: Ruined with rain. Day spent mending boat. Came on to blow in night. Had to moor boat to an anchor which continually dragged. Three times we had to turn out in the night, got soaked with rain and sea up to our waists and thus made our sleeping-bags wet when we got back in them. Tarpaulin blew off our luggage so all our spare clothes got soaked as well. *25 September*: Ditto: nothing but repairs and getting wet and cold. *26 September*: Ditto. It is getting sickening to the point of desperation. Not only have we rain to contend with… but the engine always refuses to work when it is fine, and there is always too much swell when it does work. Added to this the boat still leaks like a sieve. Today we cannot get at her to haul her out as an iceberg has sat on the mooring rope. We have finished the last bit of seal Gino shot the other day but we still have some seagulls. *27 September*: Too much swell… *28 September*. Got packed up for starting but we found the ice too tight to get on and fog thick… It really begins to look like having to winter.

The following day they got away at last. Then the motor broke down. Lemon worked on it for a whole day in such foul temper Courtauld found it nerve-wracking to be near him… and could not fix it. He announced that the only option now was to strip down the engine but the spanners he had didn't fit the nuts. It would take him two weeks to file them down to size. Gino was standing on a rock watching Lemon's efforts. Courtauld had never seen him look so depressed. 'I can see him now in his sealskin boots and brown sweater, with his hair very untidy and his face very red, looking furiously at the engine, then at the sea which sparkled blue and grinning round the rocks where he stood.' Then Courtauld had an inspiration. Into his mind entered a thought which, though mechanical rather than metaphysical, surely came from that same source which had preserved him on the ice cap. Stepping to the engine he used one of Lemon's discarded spanners to remove the silencer. He pulled the starter cord. The motor roared into exuberant healthy life.

The spirits of the three men soared. From gloom to lively action was but a moment. They piled into the boat and pushed off. It was leaking so fast one of them had to bail without cease, and another to stay aboard each night to keep it afloat. But the motor was roaring like a young lion and going great. On 1 October they covered fifty miles. On the fifth they sailed through the sound which cuts through Cape Farewell, the southern point of Greenland. They saw green fields, cows, sheep. Two days later they reached Julianehaab.

So Courtauld had made it. The ice had not caught him for another winter. There was a cargo ship in the harbour and he was free to go home and marry Mollie. Except that he was not. Before he could reach that happy end he was destined to go through yet another trial. At Julianehaab Gino learned that Rymill and Hampton, who had set off from base to cross the ice cap, were three weeks overdue on their crossing; they had not arrived at Holsteinsborg.

Lemon, who was on loan to the Air-Route Expedition from the Army, had to rejoin his regiment and took the cargo ship for England, but Gino asked Courtauld to accompany him 500 miles up the coast to form a search party for the missing men. 'There have been some hard things to bear in the last year,' Courtauld wrote to Mollie. 'But the hardest of all was this last… to see the ship sail for home and not be able to go in her.'

He and Gino set off for Holsteinsborg by trading boat. The day before they got there Rymill and Hampton came into the settlement after a journey whose last stage by kayak (carried on the sledges which they dumped) had all but drowned them when both had been swept beneath the ice. There was a ship at Holsteinsborg, about to return to Denmark. No berths were available but Gino used his charm. Money changed hands, though not much. When the *Hans Egede* sailed a few days later the four explorers were on board.

Three weeks before this Gino had sent letters to his family and Nanny which Lemon took with him to mail on his arrival in England. To his sister Pam he wrote, 'I can't tell you how sad I am not to be coming back on this boat... it is wretched. I am pretty certain (Rymill and Hampton) will turn up all right. However, as leader I can't leave.' In the letter to his father he said, 'I am longing to get home... however there is no alternative... Could you see that a complete suit – bowler hat, shoes, umbrella etc is sent to the Hotel Angleterre, Copenhagen, as I have got absolutely nothing to wear...'

Unnecessary as the Dead

A MAGNIFICENTLY UNIFORMED brass band was playing the Danish national anthem and the welcoming crowd stood bareheaded as the tall, three-masted ship steamed slowly into Copenhagen. It made fast alongside the main quay where a reception platform had been set up, draped in gaily coloured bunting. Assembled upon it to greet the Air-Route Expedition's party and their leader on their return stood formally dressed dignitaries of the Danish government wearing top hats. With them were Scott, Pam Watkins and Nanny, who had driven out from England in Riley's old four-seater. Around the base of the dais crowded the press, photographers in flat caps, newsreel film crews with box-like cameras on stout wooden tripods, and the welcoming public.

The brass band crashed into 'God Save the King' as Gino walked off the ship onto the gangway leading from its deck to the reception platform. Alerted to this official welcome by a wireless message from a newspaper, he had arranged for a suitcase packed by Nanny to be brought out by the pilot boat. He was faultlessly dressed in a pale grey, double-breasted suit, carrying a bowler hat and rolled umbrella. The other explorers, who in the flare and sizzle of flashbulbs followed him onto the platform, were picturesquely costumed in the distressed sealskin trousers and hunting anoraks they had worn for weeks, and bore with them the authentic odour of the Arctic detectable by all.

Gino gave a short diffident speech saying how happy they were to be back safe, and thanking Denmark for the support given to the expedition. After him came the head of the British Legation who at rather greater length expressed his and the explorers' fulsome thanks to the Danish government and nation for rescuing Mr Courtauld... who he now asked to say a few words himself. Courtauld did so; and as he stepped to the microphone it was plain that he was very angry indeed. He began forcefully, 'I only want to say that everything the last speaker has told you is entirely wrong. *I was not rescued by anyone...*' He detested this spotlight on him; celebrity was alien to him, to all of them. Understatement was not a manner; it was part of their nature. It went with the times as its opposite accompanies our own.

The succession of speakers on the platform came to an end. Gino excused himself to the group of officials and press saying, 'I must go and greet my Nanny who has come to meet me,' and went to join her and his sister at the back of the stage. Then the group of explorers in their stale filthy clothes completed a final trek all of fifty yards across the quay to enter the ornate, wedding-cake façade of the Hotel Angleterre where they were shown to the luxurious rooms which had been reserved for them, each with its own marble bathroom and huge wrought-iron tub on lions' feet, unlimited quantities of scalding-hot water and pile of clean, white, fluffy towels.

Bliss... but they could not soak for long. That same day they had to attend an official lunch, a reception tea, a dinner and a dance, for which they were dressed in haphazardly-fitting evening clothes hastily assembled for them – except for Gino who, thanks to Nanny, was irritatingly impeccable as ever. Their welcome and the celebration continued in a happy glow until, well after midnight, Gino gave Scott the sign and they slipped away. Scott took him to a nightclub he had found out about from the hall porter, which stayed open until breakfast. The joint was plushy and pinkly lit, warm and welcoming to a pair of explorers mildly warmed already. A band was playing the latest show tunes from America – the first time Gino had heard them. A number of smartly dressed, unattended young women were hanging around at the bar, who soon became friends. Scott remembers everyone was cheered by Gino's continually repeated phrase, 'I'm rich, I'll pay.' A round of drinks was sent over to the band, together with requests. The new numbers from America played again, followed by earlier hits which Gino and Scott had last heard on the scratchy, worn-out records at the base hut. Perhaps it was this association that caused the two men, surrounded by party-minded hostesses, to feel themselves not in the joyous present but geographically displaced.

Gino was talking of the long boat journey he had made with Courtauld and Lemon down the coast of east Greenland. This was his first opportunity to describe it to Scott, one of the few men able to comprehend its true significance. Taking a minimum of stores, they had lived from hunting and the sea. They had learned to live how the Eskimos live and to have need of nothing else, except matches. It was the ideal method of summer travel, Gino believed. In this way they could make a journey around the whole perimeter of the Arctic Circle, taking two or three years to circumnavigate the continent. With a boat, kayaks and hunting gear, a party could be self-sufficient and live indefinitely in the Arctic. 'It was not a hard life which he painted,' says Scott, 'but a real one – vivid, unfettered, full of contrasts and achievement. Suddenly he broke off, startled and embarrassed: "My God, this is a pretty poor way to spend one's first night in civilisation." He jumped up, found a partner and began to dance...'

When he returned to London, Gino moved into the hotel in South Kensington where Pam, Tony and Nanny were now resident, for their lease on the house in Onslow Crescent had come to an end and they were temporarily homeless. Colonel Watkins was also staying there, for he was taking a break from his sanatorium existence in Switzerland to be part of Gino's welcome. As a manner of life it was even more feckless than before, for the small capital remaining to them as a family after their father's extravagances had all but disappeared in the stock market collapse of two years before. As usual they were broke.

A few days after the explorers' return Stephen Courtauld gave a banquet for them. Gino was seated next to a tall, blonde young woman with cropped hair named Margot Graham. Witty, adventurous and well-travelled, she held a pilot's licence and drove a Lancia sports convertible. Someone who knew them both thought they would like each other, and they did.

The banquet at the Mayfair Hotel was a grand occasion. Above the long table where the explorers sat in tuxedos among the other guests hung the expedition's flag, a polar bear with wings, alongside the tattered Union Jack from the ice cap station, while below these banners sugar dogs hauled sweetmeat sledges across the white damask ice cap. Thoughtful planning had gone into this dinner. The menu was in Eskimo, a language at times much more complex than our own, whose subtlety was capable of defining with five different words the escalating levels of putrescence in a not yet fully table-rotten guillemot but did not possess even approximate translations for:

Hors d'Oeuvre Suedoise
Tortue Claire
Supremes de Sole au vin du Rhin
Selle de Pre-Sale aux Laitues a la Greque
Poularde au Paprika Rose
Ecrivisses a la Muscoxite
Parfat au trois coleurs
Champagne, vins divers, cognac, liqueurs

Just before Christmas, Gino was summoned to Buckingham Palace for an audience with the King. As he did not own the formal clothes required, he rented morning dress from Moss Bros, where he was insistent on just the right fit, but provided his own top hat and umbrella. He was fresh-faced, clean-shaven, slim as a schoolboy. 'He looked very young' says his father, who drove him to the interview. When they arrived in front of the palace the Coldstream Guards (Colonel Watkins' own regiment) were on ceremonial parade, mounting guard at the gate, watched by a crowd of spectators. Gino clutched his father's arm saying, 'For God's sake drive me in Daddy'; so in they drove. For Colonel Watkins this was an ironic moment in a defective parenthood, for he had had little influence on Gino's life, and that had been, as he freely admitted, negative. 'You can imagine my feelings... I thought of my disappointment when Gino was not keen to join the regiment, a disappointment which landed him at the age of twenty-four inside the Palace with the King, and me outside, the proudest man in England.' That was a significant day for Gino too, for the same evening he gave a lecture about the Air-Route Expedition to the Royal Geographical Society. The new hall was crowded to capacity with Fellows, members of the government, bankers and guests, including his family and Margot Graham. His talk, quiet, deprecating and often funny, was followed by others. Among these, J. M. Wordie alluded to the

purpose behind this gathering of eminent people when he spoke of
the enthusiasm of all there at Gino's achievement in opening up an
intercontinental airway to the US and their wish to see him setting
out on another expedition as soon as possible. But the veteran
Danish explorer Lauge Koch touched on the all too real *non-Arctic*
problem threatening this plan, and indeed the western world, not
least those in that very audience.

'Take care of Mr Watkins and his companions,' he said. 'I
beg you not to misunderstand my words. Perhaps you do
not think after hearing tonight about the experiences of the
expedition... there is any need to take care of them. But
time is short... employ them while they are young in spite of
economic questions and other difficulties.'

The England that Gino and his party of explorers returned to was a
very different place from the country they had left eighteen months
before. A blight had fallen across the world during their absence in
the Arctic: the Great Depression. Throughout the previous decade
of the Roaring Twenties in which they had come to adulthood the
economy had continued to expand (in the US absolutely, while in
the UK there had been blips). The shops were filled with fashionable
clothes, appliances and consumer goods never seen before. Jazz and
dancing set the mood and people believed the boom would go on
for ever, indeed that it was not a boom but no less than the modern
era. The music was playing and the good times rolled; there seemed
no cause why they should stop.

In America – and to a somewhat lesser extent in Britain – specu-
lation in stocks and shares became first a wheeze, then a profitable
gamble, then a mania. Everyone knew of someone who had become
a millionaire, and people bought on margin with money they didn't
have – and showed a profit. But the health of the banking system was

pathologically unsound; false prophets, shysters and bunko artists had infiltrated and corrupted the market, as happens in times of plenty. A few months before the explorers' departure for Greenland, a London banking house had failed; its owner was convicted of forgery and sent to jail. Then on the fateful date of 29 October 1929 the towering edifice of inflated prices began to crumble and collapse beneath its own weight. The dream, that wondrous vision of Utopia people believed was real, disintegrated before their eyes and revealed itself as dust. By 11.30 that day the New York market was in freefall, gripped by blind panic. Outside the Exchange in Broad Street groups of traumatised people came together in a crowd. A noise was coming off them that was not recognisable as human. The sound emitting from that stricken herd penetrated the walls of the Exchange building to reach those cowering within as an animal howl of baffled pain.

While Gino and his carefree band had been adventuring in the north, not just the mood but the very look of England had been transformed. Coal mines, dockyards and mills had shut down, hundreds of thousands of men and women were thrown out of work. At first the unemployed had been jokey and defiant, but by now idleness and poverty had withered their spirit. Everything they owned had been pawned, even their clothes had gone into hock. Outside closed pits men picked over slag heaps, at nightfall wheeling home a filthy sack slung across the handlebars of a bicycle. Throughout the country were hunger marches, soup lines, dole queues. Sullen, slope-shouldered men in flat caps slouched at street corners in hopeless apathy. The spectral shadows of the past reappeared to haunt the towns: starvation, malnutrition, tuberculosis. In their streets embittered, worn-out women shrieked in fury at screaming children dressed in rags. The England that the explorers returned home to had become a bleak and ruined land.

Scott wrote of the New Year of 1932:

> When the flush of home-coming is gone there often follows a
> numbing sense of flatness and despondency. In a far country
> men have struggled after an objective which seemed entirely
> worth the price of cold, of hunger and of fear. They have
> achieved it and come back triumphant to find that England
> has dutifully praised them, and quite failed to appreciate that
> life has gone on and they must hurry to catch up with it. These
> stay-at-homes have only lived one life, the reasonable life.
> Their questions are foolish, then annoying; their indifference
> is galling, and even their praise seems patronising. The
> inability to accept... a completely different sense of values has
> driven returning wanderers to seek their own lives, finding
> themselves as unnecessary as the dead...

That untidy room overlooking the park in the RGS, which Gino still
used as an office, became a drop-in centre for returned explorers
where they composed CVs and job applications, lounged about,
talked and played the gramophone. But the job market did not
exist: across the board employers were cutting back, not hiring.
Some of the men had brought their kayaks with them on the ship
to England and one day to cheer themselves up they strapped these
onto their cars and drove to a pub on the Thames where they
competed against each other on the current and practised rolling
them as they had learned from the Eskimos. Gino had invited
Margot Graham along to watch. Afterwards she raced him back to
London; her Lancia against the two-seater Morris he had bought
for a few pounds within days of getting home. Not surprisingly
she was the winner in her more powerful machine, despite Gino's
reckless challenge. 'Driving with him very fast in an unstable almost
brakeless vehicle, one scarcely had time to relax after escaping one

collision before one was gripping the door in anticipation of the next,' Scott says. He was always running out of petrol. 'Does it need oil as well?' he asked one of his more mechanically minded friends. 'It's so expensive and I don't know where to put it in. I've never looked under the bonnet.'

Despite the distraction of a budding love affair, Gino was soon immersed again in work. The Air-Route Expedition had received considerable media coverage. He and Courtauld were stars (with Courtauld hating every minute of it).

The King: I am sure you were very cold, Mr Courtauld?
Courtauld: No sir.
The King: You were hungry though?
Courtauld: No sir.
The King: You must have felt desperately lonely?
Courtauld: No sir.
The King: I am very glad to give you the Polar Medal.

That was the extent of the exchange between the two when the monarch invested him, Gino and Scott with the award. But Gino knew that celebrity has a shelf life – he must act while he was still hot if he was to raise money for a new expedition.

His first plan was to spend three years travelling around the coasts which rim the Arctic Circle, supporting his party by hunting and wintering where the season halted them. J. M. Wordie and Professor Debenham, who had been south with Scott and Shackleton – an experience which had left them curiously streetwise – both counselled against the project. This expedition should be bigger and more important than the last, they advised. To obtain funding it must capture the public imagination. The still-unknown areas of the world were few; the great geographical problem yet to be solved lay not to the north but in the Antarctic.

Going south did not appeal to Gino. The Antarctic was comprised of five million square miles of ice where there were no Eskimos and hunting involved only clubbing to death helpless penguins who had never seen man and thought he was their friend. Nevertheless he saw the point of his mentors' argument and its expediency. The map of the world was all but filled in. The last remaining puzzle was whether the Antarctic was indeed a continent – or two vast islands. At present the map of the Antarctic showed two huge bays on its opposing coasts: the Ross Sea and the Weddell Sea. Did these two 'bays' in fact *connect*?

By a journey of 1,500 miles over unmapped, unknown but emphatically hostile country Gino proposed to discover the answer. He put his plan to the Royal Geographical Society, who approved it. The scheme meant leaving England that autumn in order to make the attempt during the Antarctic summer. As with Scott and Shackleton's expeditions, there would be national prestige attached to this one. Its members would be British and it must be a British ship that carried them. Only one was available, the *Discovery*, the large 500-ton wooden vessel in which Scott had sailed to the Antarctic in 1901.

Inevitably Gino's plans were picked up by the press, who pounced on the story: *Youngest British Explorer to chart Antarctic Wastes ... Last Riddle ... Intrepid Young Leader ... Silent White Lands ...* In these grim days of soup-lines and cheerless winter, the reports painted a vivid picture of a young leader and his companions setting south on a bold venture aboard an historic ship with two airplanes lashed upon the deck. Yet all this was but a dream which Gino was trying to shape into some sort of reality.

By now Gino, Pam, Tony and Nanny were living in a rented house in Hill Street, Mayfair, which they had moved into when Colonel Watkins returned to Switzerland. Gino described their life there in a letter to his father: 'So far all is going well... although the cook has threatened to leave once or twice she has not done so yet. Of course Nanny has already taken over the food supply and the cook decides how many people we may invite in during the week and Nanny decides who these people must be. Apart from that we entirely run the house ourselves.'

There and in his office in the RGS, both of which were always crowded with people, Gino concentrated on his new expedition. 'Then with the full drive of his amazing energy he began his search for money,' says Scott. At any time it was uncongenial work, but now it was discouraging as well. In spite of his far greater reputation, the task before him was infinitely more difficult than it had been two years before. It was the worst of times. Previously prosperous and secure people were now merely hanging on. No business was doing well – except the cinema, the one escape into a richer world. Gino went to see many people and convinced many of the soundness of his plans, but beyond that he could not go. 'In the depths of the Depression private finance was more surely frozen than the ice of the Antarctic,' Scott wrote.

It was discouraging to come up against so many refusals and, as spring turned to early summer in 1932, it got to Gino. Not that many observed it for his façade remained good; he could always put on a show for the world to see. But Nanny, who could 'read him like a book', noticed a change in him. She had known him since infancy and what she saw now bothered her. Others observed only that he seemed preoccupied and spent more time alone working in his room.

Many people were preoccupied at that time. Britain had gone off the gold standard and there was talk of a complete collapse in the economic system. No one knew quite what that meant but the scenario was scary. Even as things were the Watkins' situation was precarious. Gino, Tony and Pam's capital of £1,000 apiece, inherited from their mother, yielded only a tiny income and nothing could be expected of their father. One evening the three of them were discussing how long they could continue to rent the Hill Street house and what to do if it became impossible, when Gino proposed they should all move to the Arctic. There was a long, startled pause. Then to break the silence Pam asked, 'Will Nanny come too?' 'Of course, she'll look after us,' said Gino. They laughed and took it for a joke, but it was not. He saw it as a solution if things collapsed in England; he knew he could house and feed them there, free of these worldly cares. But, unsurprisingly, his family were dismayed at the notion of swapping Knightsbridge for a diet of sealmeat and life in the frozen wild. It was a grotesque suggestion; it *had* to be a joke, or else Gino's reason was slipping.

The members of the Air-Route Expedition who had come from the Army and Air Force had returned to their service and salary, but the others had not yet found work. They continued dutifully to apply for vacancies while hoping Gino's next expedition would prevent them from accepting if a job was offered. They all wanted to go back – north, south, whichever... Except possibly Scott, though he too was suffering from the same sense of displacement as the rest felt.

We all found it difficult to settle down in what had become – for all our homesick thoughts – a strange soil. This estrangement showed... We tended to hang together like fruits of the same transplanted tree. The other trees were as kind, interested and complimentary as could be but only we shared roots.

Then Captain Lemon died. During the early weeks in Greenland at the start of the expedition Lemon had taken against Gino's casual style of leadership. He was a professional soldier, disciplined and precise in his way of thinking. He considered Gino's methods amateur and slapdash, and said so. The two had a row about it, but rather than making them enemies the argument had the opposite effect. Lemon was the first to offer to accompany Gino on the boat journey to Julianehaab. 'He would have followed him anywhere, careless… whether the plans looked sound and reasonable on paper,' Scott says. After returning from the Arctic, 'He was the first apple to fall. He killed himself. There was no evident reason.'

Gino was invited to Denmark to receive the country's polar medal from Crown Prince Frederik. He stayed with the British Ambassador and the evening of the award lectured in English to an appreciative crowd of 1,500 Danes. Afterwards he was questioned about his current plans to cross the Antarctic. He answered confidently, enthusing them with the venture – but it must have been hard to do so while all too conscious of the lack of reality behind it. A number of cheques for £5 or £10 had arrived at the expedition office but, despite his weeks of canvassing, not a single corporate sponsor had come on board. The hope of sailing for the south that year was shrinking further with each day; April and May were stressful months for Gino. He was urgently following up every contact, meeting and lunching with possible sponsors. Meanwhile he travelled the country lecturing on the Air-Route Expedition in order to pay off its debts, for the accounts were in the red. 'He was working rather hectically now, for the future had become so uncertain. He could not rest,' Scott writes. 'Inevitably the Antarctic project kept him from his bed and strained his high-strung mind.' Gino asked Margot Graham to marry him. An impulsive gesture, oddly timed for a man scheming hard not to see his fiancée for the next three years. Pam and Tony were baffled by it.

As a last appeal for funds, in a letter published in *The Times* Professor Debenham wrote:

Someone is going to cross the great Antarctic continent from sea to sea and settle for ever the last great geographical problem which remains... A complacent world will then ink in the doubtful lines on its atlases ... hardly realising that an end has come to major discoveries on this globe forever and a day... Two expeditions from America have been planned for next year, the leaders being Admiral Byrd and Mr Ellsworth, both intending to make this discovery by air. For the last few months, in a small room at the Royal Geographical Society, a group of young men have been planning the same journey of 1,500 miles, not by air but on foot with dog teams... In another week it will be too late... It seems a thousand pities... [they] should be forced to give up their brave project, to abandon their hope of following in the footsteps of Scott and Wilson, "To strive, to seek, to find, and not to yield."

The letter brought in many encouraging replies and a few small cheques. It touched the heart but not the purse of any sponsor; the purses all were empty or stayed shut. 'The striving of the last five months had come to nothing,' Scott writes. Gino showed his disappointment to no one. 'He was cold as ice,' says Chapman. 'He had complete and absolute control over himself and felt it an admission of weakness to show what he felt.'

Two or three weeks before this a dubious alternative plan had been presented to Gino in the form of a very bad deal. That was not the fault of the man who brokered it, Vilhjalmur Stefansson; it was the best he could get. Stefansson was now working as an adviser to Pan American Airways, who were offering Gino a sum of £500 to continue for a further year his survey work for an air route over the ice cap. It was a lousy offer but in a sudden decision Gino now cabled Stefansson he would accept it, then sent another cable to Denmark booking four places on the *Gertrud Rask* which would sail from Copenhagen for east Greenland in the middle of July.

'I do hope Gino has made a wise decision,' his father wrote. For finance he had Pan Am's £500, £200 from the RGS, £100 from *The Times*, who bought the Press rights to the expedition such as it was, plus the personal cheques which had dribbled in over the last few months. In all, it amounted to less than £1,000 (now about £40,000). The necessary survey and meteorological instruments he could get from the Air Ministry and RGS, but with that money he had to purchase stores and all other equipment required, ship four men to Greenland (and eventually back), buy sledges, dogs and boats and feed the party and their animals for a year. It was an inauspicious plan, yet Chapman, Riley and Rymill jumped at the chance of coming. 'I admire him and feel perfectly happy with him, and I would follow him anywhere,' Chapman wrote. But before inviting any of these three to accompany him, Gino had first asked Scott. And Scott awkwardly had refused. He couldn't come, he had been offered a job, he said. It wasn't true and Scott was a poor liar and Gino must have known it wasn't so, but all he said was, 'Pity, but keep an eye on Pam, will you.'

Scott could not face returning to the place where he had failed. What had happened on the ice cap the year before had shattered his image of himself, but in refusing to accompany Gino now, he created for himself a personal demon who would cling to his back and reproach him for the rest of his life. Until his death at the age of seventy-nine, while climbing an apple tree, he believed that if he had said yes and gone with Gino he could have changed the way the story ended.

Too Close to The Edge

On 11 July Chapman met Gino at Liverpool Street station to catch the boat train to Harwich. 'Many explorers have written of the intolerable period of reaction between expeditions,' Chapman recorded. 'In our case we had returned to civilisation, full of enthusiasm and optimism, after a year of glorious life, to find a cynical, dampening world, peopled mainly by business men, whose outlook was entirely different from our own... In Greenland we had led a life of complete freedom, hunting and contriving... at the same time feeling that our work was of real value. But in England... everything tended to fall flat.'

Margot Graham and Riley's father, who would both accompany the party as far as Copenhagen, had driven to Harwich by car. During the crossing to Denmark, Gino and Margot lay on deck together sunbathing and reading the final pages of the book on the Air-Route Expedition as Chapman struggled to complete them in the saloon. 'Jove I'm happy,' he found time to write in his diary about the prospect ahead. 'Life is just too good. What a year I shall have.'

On arrival in Denmark they found Riley and Rymill waiting for them. Two motorboats were already loaded on the tall four-masted steam schooner *Gertrud Rask,* about to set off on her annual voyage to Angmagssalik. They sailed next morning. Gino's diary takes up the story:

July 14. Well, we are off at last. It has been a hectic time. Riley and Rymill went ahead... Margy and I followed... We were surrounded by press photographers... Margy and Riley's father were allowed to come on the ship as far as Elsinore, 3½ hours. That was wonderful, as it would have been terrible saying good-bye on the crowded quay. It was wonderfully calm and hot. Margy and I sat upright in the bows watching the coast go by. At last the awful moment came. A small pilot boat came alongside and Margy and the rest had to leave. She was wonderful, but it was hell. I watched her boat glide away across the water until it was a speck in the distance. The ship is heavily loaded. Our petrol is in the bows. Next our two motorboats, then a mass of various stores, including two sledge dogs. We are all going to bed early. I have averaged 3 hours 37 minutes in bed per night for the last month. To prepare for a year's work in 5 weeks is difficult. Chapman has just come to me to say that the film camera is broken...

July 15. After 6 hours' work I have mended the camera. It was a frightful job and at one time I thought I should have to give up...

July 16-July 21. I have always hated the sea and always shall... It has been so rough that we have had to wedge ourselves into our bunks with rolled-up rugs or anything we could find... We are now coaling in Seydisfjord, Iceland. We are off again in one hour. In two days we should reach the ice pack. This is the fourth time I have come to the Arctic. It is queer how it gets hold of one, 'the call of the North.' The first time a man comes to the Arctic he probably comes half for adventure, half in pursuit of some scientific object. On his first visit he is either scared and never comes again or he gets the Arctic in him and returns again and again. In the last 5 years I have only spent about a total of 2 out of the Arctic. I suppose this is the last time that I shall be coming...

Soon after breakfast on 23 July, a white line appeared on the horizon. Ice blink! That peculiar reflection in the sky which denotes the near presence of ice. They were soon in the thick of it, crashing and grinding between the floes. 'It has been a wonderful day and we have all been sitting about in the sun on deck,' Gino writes. They were back in the perpetual day of Arctic summer, night and dark had been banished by the ever-present sun. The sky was pink and milky-blue fleeced with cloud, and the pack-ice spread into the distance as a misty radiance in which towering icebergs loomed like ships of a ghostly armada, signalling to each other through the haze with pale reflected fire.

The next morning the *Gertrud Rask* anchored in Scoresby Sound to unload a year's supplies, then sailed for Angmagssalik. They arrived in the evening. It was a rough night and raining, but many kayaks came out to meet them outside the bay, just as a school of whales went past. The first man they met nearly rolled over with excitement when he saw them. He shouted that all their old friends were in Angmagssalik. By the time they reached the settlement there were at least 100 kayaks in the water around them. Gertrude and Tina came out to meet them in a boat. They were welcomed back as members of the tribe, their return was feted. Lodged with the Eskimos for a week, sharing their distinctive meals in the familiar gamey atmosphere of the communal dwelling, passing each night in the heap of fur and bodies on the sleeping platform, they learnt everything of importance that had happened while they had been away: who had killed a polar bear, who a narwhal; who had died and who had given birth. Chapman had received news on this before anyone; before he had even stepped ashore Gertrud had introduced him to his son. 'I felt completely bowled over at first. But all is apparently well: Hansie is a fine boy and looks just like me. No one is annoyed apparently… Hansie's presence doesn't spoil her chances of marriage thank God.' When he had overcome his shock, Chapman found he was pleased by what had occurred and proud of the baby. Told by the magistrate he would have to contribute £20 a year to the cost of supporting and educating the boy, he dismissed the suggestion: 'Nonsense – he'll go to Sedbergh.'

On 9 August the *Gertrud Rask* steamed north through the pack ice to land the four explorers and an Eskimo, Karli, at Lake Fjord, together with their dogs (bought at Angmagssalik), boats, equipment and gramophone. Then she raised her anchor and left, not to return for a year. Here they set up their base camp. 'I don't think one of us felt a single pang of regret as our last link with civilisation snapped and we were thrown on our own resources. It was like the beginning of a marvellous summer holiday: the ideal sort of existence one dreamed of in boyhood,' Chapman wrote.

Lake Fjord was known to Gino. During his survey journey up the coast two years before in the *Quest* he had examined the inlet and the freshwater lake at its head, and realised this to be the natural site for an air base and refuelling point for a flight route over the ice cap. His intention this time was to survey and map the surrounding mountains and adjacent coast, and to obtain year-round meteorological records for what would eventually become an airport – hard as it was to imagine such a thing in that panorama of uninhabited mountain wilderness, savagery and desolation.

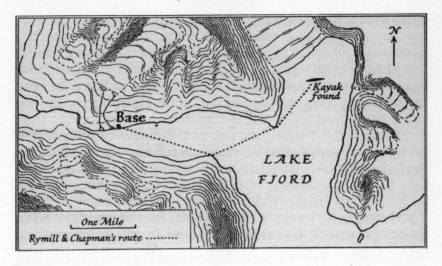

This is the place where the last act of the story is to be staged. This is the backdrop to the scene, and to follow how the action plays it is necessary to visualise the physical setting. Viewed on a map, Lake Fjord is Y-shaped. One arm of the Y is long and straight, sheltered by mountains, an ideal place for a seaplane to land in tolerable weather and westerly winds. This stretch of water ends in a green fertile valley with a stream running through it, draining from the lake above which provides an alternative landing area. It was by this river mouth that the party erected their bell tent and set up the array of meteorological instruments. But the other shorter arm of the Y is different, even forbidding in appearance. Enclosed between precipitous high black cliffs, it terminates abruptly in a vertical 100-foot wall of ice, the end point of a glacier snaking down steeply from the mountains. 'A dangerous ice-face,' Scott described it later, 'for every now and then, as the frozen river crawls ponderously towards the sea, a piece large or small is carved off from its termination and falls with a roar into the water to send waves chasing each other down the bay.'

Having set up their camp the party go to work at once, adjusting their routine to the rhythm of a twenty-two hour day. Riley occupies himself with the meteorological instruments, Rymill and Chapman go off surveying, Karli the Eskimo minds house and cooks. It is Gino's job to hunt. They have brought only basics with them – and little enough of these because of lack of money. They must lay in all the food they and their dogs will need for the year before the ice begins to re-form and days shorten to winter night. On 11 August at 10 a.m. Gino launches his kayak and heads out towards the mouth of the fjord...

Solitude and silence all around save for the cry of seabirds. The sea is a dark green mirror below the black fortress wall of the cliffs and the white kayak slices across its glassy sheen in a swift clean line, cutting along the lanes of dark water between the ice floes. Man and craft are enclosed in a translucent radiance of sunlight flaring from the crystal facets of the floating ice. Gino's harpoon is strapped by him on deck, his loaded rifle in its holster beside it. He is back in an elemental world and life is wonderfully simplified. He is hunting for prey, for food to feed his tribe. Wholly intent on what he is engaged in, there is no space in his mind for other thoughts; his focus is total.

12 August: I go out hunting. Have an exciting time with a seal. About 1 hour to kill. It pulls bladder right under water. Comes up under kayak. Strain wrist pulling it home. Seven fish in seine net. 13 August: Fog outside so do not seal hunt; fish, and dry fish and skin seal. Got 30 fish in the net. My wrist is bad. 14 August: Rymill and I both decided to hunt today. I bandaged my wrist tightly and put iodine on it. Rymill took the south side of the fjord and I took the north. I went up to the glacier and paddled along about 100 yards from it. I saw a seal and harpooned it very close to the glacier. Luckily it was almost dead and I towed it out of the danger zone. Then I had a very narrow escape. I got out on an ice floe with my kayak and started to blow up the seal. I was about 20 yards

from the cliffs and ¼ mile from the glacier. Suddenly a large piece broke off the glacier. I knew what would happen and seized a piece of line and fastened it to my kayak. Suddenly the wave reached me and the floe was carried against the cliffs and broken up. I clung on to a ledge. My kayak was turned over and all the hunting gear carried away. Luckily I managed to collect everything. On the way home the ice started to close in but I got through all right.

The next day and the day following he tries to hunt but there is too much ice in the fjord. The day after is also unsuitable for hunting, but Gino and Rymill catch fifty fish in their net in one haul. Ice blocks the fjord the morning after, so they devote their time to filming Chapman stalking a musk ox. On 19 August, Gino's diary records: 'I went out at 11 to hunt but had no luck. Shot one seal and missed with my harpoon.'

That is the last entry. They intended next morning to do more filming but when Riley gets up at five to make porridge, the sky is overcast and dull. So, instead, Chapman and Rymill go off in the motor boat to continue surveying the fjord, while Gino leaves in his kayak at the same time to hunt, headed for the short arm of the fjord below the glacier which is the most likely place to find seals and where he had narrowly escaped drowning six days before.

The two surveyors spend about three hours up on the shore of the other fjord, taking bearings and calculating distances with the range finder. While doing so they hear a crash of ice splitting from the glacier two miles away, but recall this only later for these ice-falls are quite usual. At noon they cross in the boat to the point separating the two sections of the fjord and make more observations there, then start across the short arm of the Y where Chapman spots something in the sea ahead. Drawing closer, they see it is a white kayak floating upside down. Emptying it of water, they lift it on board. The harpoon is still strapped in place but the throwing stick is missing. The gun too is gone from its holster. Worried, the two men scan the water and shoreline through binoculars. They stop the motor and shout Gino's name into the silence; the tall cliffs throw back its echo. Restarting the engine they sail the length of the fjord to beneath the glacier wall and run the length of it. They see a dark shape on one of the small ice floes which turns out to be Gino's trousers and kayak belt. They have thawed a hollow in the ice, so must have been there for several hours.

Clearly there has been an accident. Anxiously they try to reconstruct what has happened. Possibly he got out of the kayak to shoot a seal or rearrange his hunting gear when the glacier calved and the wave swept his craft away. Perhaps he removed his heavy clothing to dive in and swim to recover his kayak. Perhaps the ice fall capsized him and in the turbulence he lost both paddle and throwing stick. But why had he not been able to right the craft by hand alone? Had he extricated himself from the kayak but been unable to scramble onto the floe? Thrown his trousers on the ice then tried to swim to shore? 'It seemed incredible,' Chapman writes. 'He seemed invulnerable. He dwelt apart and seemed not to be ruled by ordinary laws. Yet...'

Perhaps Gino had reached the shore and walked home barefoot across the mountains. They sail back to base only to meet Riley and Karli in the dinghy, who stare in shock at the sight of Gino's kayak on their deck. Picking up blankets, a thermos and the medicine kit, they quarter the fjord again. Chapman and Rymill take ropes and ice axes, climb the glacier and search the route home. They search until midnight. They search all next day. But Gino has gone. 'He was always appropriate,' says Scott, 'and it was right that none should see him dead.'

Chapman writes:

It was a heavenly night. With the ageless pinnacle of Ingolf silhouetted against the bright yellow and orange of the fading sunset, with hard purple clouds above. A half moon rose higher and higher over the sea, and the stars were almost dimmed by the shaking curtain of aurora, at first a nebulous radiance but gradually changing to clear-cut ribbons of light quivering and waving like seaweed fixed to a rock in a strong tide. I saw Auriga and Lyra, the Pleiades and Cygnus, all going round the Pole Star just as if nothing had happened – and Gino is dead in the fjord. How shall we carry on without his inspiration? I can't grasp the fullness of the tragedy – he might have done so much, and he is dead.

He was twenty-five years old.

Stoic Code

Y OU DON'T BLUB, *you do not break down; even in extremis or the worst of circumstances you endeavour to remain always the same man. You stiffen the upper lip and carry on.* That was the code Chapman, Riley and Rymill had been raised with.

After Gino's disappearance that is how they behaved. During the days that followed reason told them he was gone, yet secretly each believed that he could not really be dead. Suppressing all emotion in the way they had been taught, they carried on as though nothing had happened. His name came up often in their conversation but quite naturally they spoke of him in the present tense. All caught themselves at moments glancing furtively toward the bare heights at the fjord's mouth, expecting against all the laws of possibility to see his slender figure walking toward them, apologising for his lateness and lack of shoes. He would want to wash and change before amusing them with the tale of his misadventure over dinner.

Rymill took over leadership of the party, as he was the eldest. It took them two days to sail in the whale boat to Angmagssalik, where they reported Gino's death to the magistrate and the settlement's

Eskimos, who wept when they heard it. From the radio station they sent a cable in morse to the expedition committee at the RGS, asking them to break the news to Gino's fiancée and family. They transmitted a long despatch to *The Times* and another to Stefansson at Pan-American Airways in which they requested authorisation to continue the work of the expedition, mapping the air route. A couple of days later Stephansson cabled Pan-Am's approval.

So they sailed north in the whale boat and carried on the work. They continued with it until the end of summer. One day in early August they were in the boat taking depth-soundings off Lake Fjord when the silence was shattered by a noise so incongruous and unexpected it was a moment before they identified what it was that caused it. A single-wing seaplane (a Lockhead Vega, the most sleekly beautiful aircraft ever built) swooped low from the north, banked steeply to circle around them as pilot and co-pilot waved in greeting from its open cockpits, then continued on its journey south. The explorers met the couple a few days later at Angmagssalik where they had landed in the harbour. It was Colonel Lindbergh (first man to fly London–Paris five years before, and now like themselves working for Pan-Am) with his wife in their own monoplane. They had just flown the ice cap, crossing it from Holsteinsborg on the west coast in under five hours. In notable contrast to their own experiences on that same route, the couple had had an easy flight and enjoyed a picnic on the way across.

A road had been laid across the sky, linking America to Europe, but it was no highway. For the aircraft of the period with their primitive instruments of navigation, compasses subject to gross error, and whose maximum altitude was limited, it constituted a very dangerous ill-conditioned road, for most 'weather' is found below 6,000 feet. During World War II the path was flown by ferry-pilots (several of them young women) delivering US bombers to airfields in England. A number of them did not make it to their destination.

The war enormously accelerated aircraft technology and design; at its end the long-range bombers then in production were converted into passenger planes and given the name 'airliners'. A key moment in transatlantic air service occurred in June 1945 when the US Civil Aeronautics Board granted permission to three carriers to operate services across the north Atlantic; these were Pan-Am, TWA and American Export Airlines. American Export were first off the mark; by October they were offering a regular passenger service from New York to Hurn Airport (near Bournemouth in England).

So, as Chapman, Riley and Rymill wound up their expedition and prepared to leave Greenland at the end of the summer 1932, despite the tragedy of Gino's death, they had accomplished what they had set out to do: they had linked Europe to the US and opened up the world. What they had done, despite the adversities they had encountered, was in its understated, very English way – and how they would have hated the word – heroic.

Yet time changes all things, and the subtext to life's story invariably proves to be ironic. That bunch of clean-shaven young chaps with combed-flat hair would be mortified to learn that today they have morphed into inadvertent scoundrels who stand in their sealskin trousers bewildered at the bar of history, for they brought to East Greenland not just the Charleston but 'civilisation' and cued the process that ruined the Eskimos as a race, making them dependent on the food, articles and values that *we* hold good. The effect was swift: all too soon the ability to construct an igloo, drive dogs, build or handle a kayak and hunt was lost. A hamburger was tastier than a lump of blubber, and liquor was good too.

And that's not all. These prisoners arraigned in the dock stand indicted on a further charge. Their expedition to pioneer a route between Europe and America prompted an intercontinental traffic which would carve broad corridors through the Arctic sky along which giant charabancs replete with passengers power their noxious way above Greenland, discharging a pall of toxic waste upon an ice cap which has started to melt. The heroes of this period tale have become the villains.

In September, Chapman, Riley and Rymill struck camp and left Angmagssalik in a sailing schooner to arrive in Iceland a week later, just in time to catch the regular steamer to Hull in the north of England. It was a bleak grey world they came home to. The Great Depression had spread across the US and Europe like a degenerative disease; this was the depth of the slump. Small wiry men with pinched faces slouched idly on street corners or stood in shabby hopeless groups outside the Labour Exchange staring blankly into camera. England was a place of bitterness, protest marches and demonstrations broken up by police on horseback wielding long sticks; a country administered ineptly by a National Government of complacent elderly men empty of ideas. 'A land of snobbery and privilege ruled largely by the old and silly,' as George Orwell put it. A land in which there was no work, no hope, no future. What was there here for those returning from that glorious place where they had lived?

Two years before, a party of young men had sailed for the Arctic aboard the *Quest* in a spirit of light-hearted adventure. All were altered by what they found there and within themselves. Along with the rest, Scott never adjusted to everyday life. 'Look after Pam,' Gino had said to him. Scott had a strong sense of duty; that too was part of the manly code. The year after Gino's death he married Pam. It was a disastrous mistake for both of them for they had nothing whatever in common except, in time, three sons, the eldest of them myself. During World War II Scott trained special forces in irregular warfare, survival and silent killing. After that he worked abroad, then for the *Daily Telegraph*. He wrote books. In the course of his life he published thirty-five, two of them bestsellers. Yet nothing gave him happiness. He hated family life, ties, responsibilities, job, routine. Only when trekking alone in rough country could he feel at ease within himself. In the Arctic he had found the only existence that delivered.

Courtauld, like Scott, peaked in the Arctic. Within weeks of his return he married Mollie, the first and only woman in his life, but remained restless and could not settle. He devised an act of homage to his lost leader: 'I thought I would get up an expedition to have a stab at the mountains Gino had discovered.' Since he had first seen the unknown range, Dutch, French and Italian expeditions had failed in their attempts to climb it. In 1935 he chartered the *Quest* and sailed to Greenland with a party which included Mollie and two Everest mountaineers. They had success: 'Got peak yesterday,' he reports. It proved to be the highest mountain in Greenland, as Gino had guessed it to be when he first saw it.

That was Courtauld's last expedition. There followed a large country house, six children, a dull war and a dull peace – his only excitement sailing – never a job, never fitting in, a millionaire misfit, disinterested and at peace. Courageous always, for although the ice failed to get him, multiple sclerosis progressively froze his limbs until no muscle remained, but to the end he would have his arms lashed to the wheel of his racing yacht so that he might sail it in a high wind. He had never wished to be a hero and his assessment of himself is characteristic: 'Just an ordinary chap.'

'Why do I want to be famous?' Chapman wrote in his Greenland diary. He did not answer the question but it was clear both to himself and others that he was hungry for fame. He succeeded in this ambition. At the start of the war, he, like Scott, trained Special Forces in guerrilla tactics, then was landed by submarine behind Japanese lines in Malaya to spend three and a half years in the jungle organising disruption and chaos. It is recorded that during one fortnight he cut the railway line in sixty places, blew up fifteen bridges, destroyed forty trucks and killed or wounded several hundred Japanese soldiers. He was awarded the DSO and Bar. After the war he married, fathered three sons, founded a school and sought to inspire its pupils with 'the spirit of adventure' which had informed his own life. Some *were* inspired by him but others mocked. Attitudes had changed. In time illness fingered him. He suffered from stomach pain and his prostate troubled him; it was humiliating. Since childhood he had defined himself by heroic endeavour. With marriage and children, with a job and insufficient income, with age and the infirmities that come with age, heroic endeavour becomes harder to achieve. 'I fear that one day I may incontinently shoot myself,' he had written while still an undergraduate; at the age of sixty-four he did so.

But Chapman also wrote, 'I do not think any part of my life could have been happier than those years in Greenland.' He, Courtauld and Scott were changed forever by the Arctic – by what each had experienced there, and by Gino, their inspiration. He had led them into a magical domain, a more vital level of reality where they had lived and felt and had their youthful being in finer light, brighter and more exalted air. Their senses had been forced wide open; in body, mind and spirit they were one.

What they had tasted there was a pure rush. They were addicted to that vast empty place of cruel beauty and truth. To face the adversities they encountered had required comradeship, resolution and courage; their lives were simple, their purpose clear. In that bare white world of elemental simplicity their existence had a heroic purity and nothing later could come close to it. What remained afterwards was a leftover life to live; it could never be that good again. Only Gino departed at the top. In Scott's words: 'He never intended to come back.'

NOTE ON SOURCES

Throughout this book, Jeremy Scott has quoted extensively from contemporary sources, including the books, journals and letters of the explorers themselves. He has also drawn upon other books of exploration and anthropology. A complete list of these sources follows herewith.

Readers who would like more information on the extracts quoted by Jeremy Scott in *Dancing on Ice* are invited to address their queries to the author, care of Old Street Publishing.

Northern Lights, F. Spencer Chapman, Chatto and Windus 1932

Watkins' Last Expedition, F. Spencer Chapman, Chatto and Windus 1934

Helvellyn to Himalaya, F. Spencer Chapman, Chatto and Windus 1940

Living Dangerously, F. Spencer Chapman, Chatto and Windus 1953

Gino Watkins, J. M. Scott, Hodder and Stoughton 1935

The Private Life of Polar Exploration, J. M. Scott, William Blackwood 1982

The Man on the Icecap, Nicholas Wollaston, Constable 1980

One Man's Jungle, Ralph Barker, Chatto and Windus 1975

Those Greenland Days, Martin Lindsay, Penguin 1939

Three Got Through, Martin Lindsay, Youth Book Club 1950

The Last Kings of Thule, Jean Malaurie, Jonathan Cape 1983

The Friendly Arctic, Vilhjalmur Stefansson, Macmillan 1921

My Life with the Eskimo, Vilhjalmur Stefansson, Collier Books 1966

ACKNOWLEDGEMENTS

I WOULD LIKE to thank a number of people who have contributed in various ways to the birth of this book: first, Julian Friedmann and Chloe Benedictus at Blake Friedmann for their professionalism, exemplary patience and good nature.

Also Sally Abbey, Freddie Ahad, the Venerable John Barton, Eddie Canton, Ernest and Christie Chapman, Helen Dawes, Andrew Franklin, Ben and Bridget Fisher, James Garrett, Christine Groom, Martin Howells, Sue Jackson, Cassandra Jardine, James and Chris Macdonald, Dr Paul and Wendi MacLoughlin, Jennie McClean, John Mason, Peter Nichols, Felicie Oakes, Bob Old, Mark Ramage, David Scott, Hamish and Stephanie Scott, Sasha Scott, Adriana Scott, Michael Shearing, Lee Shearing, Ben Sherward, Alan and Diane Spiegelman, Vivien Tyler, Jonothan Watkins, Richard Watkins, Marian Whitehouse, Sir Brian Wilson.

Lastly: Sam Carter, Ben and Francesca Yarde-Buller and Sarah Wray.